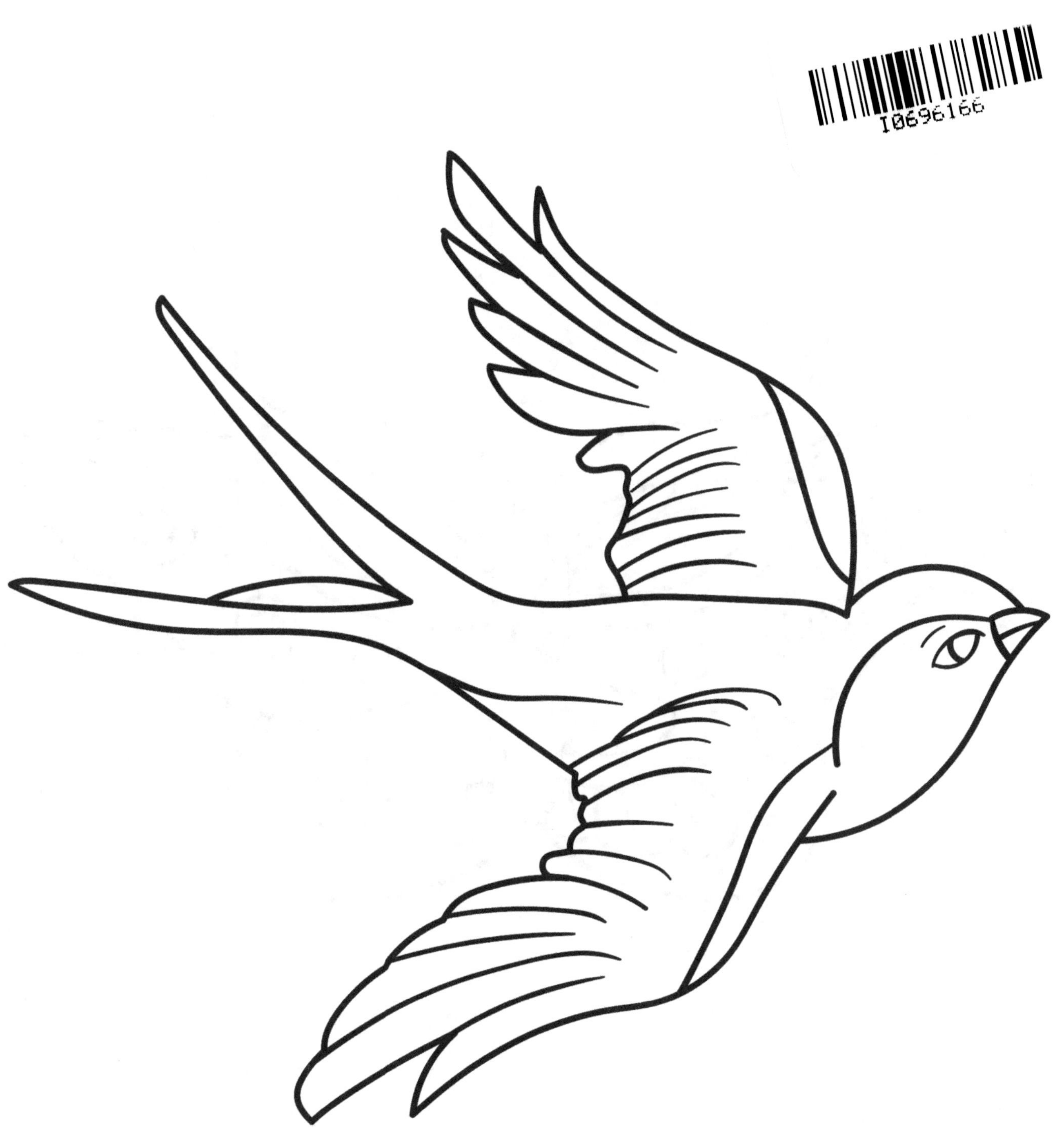
I0696166

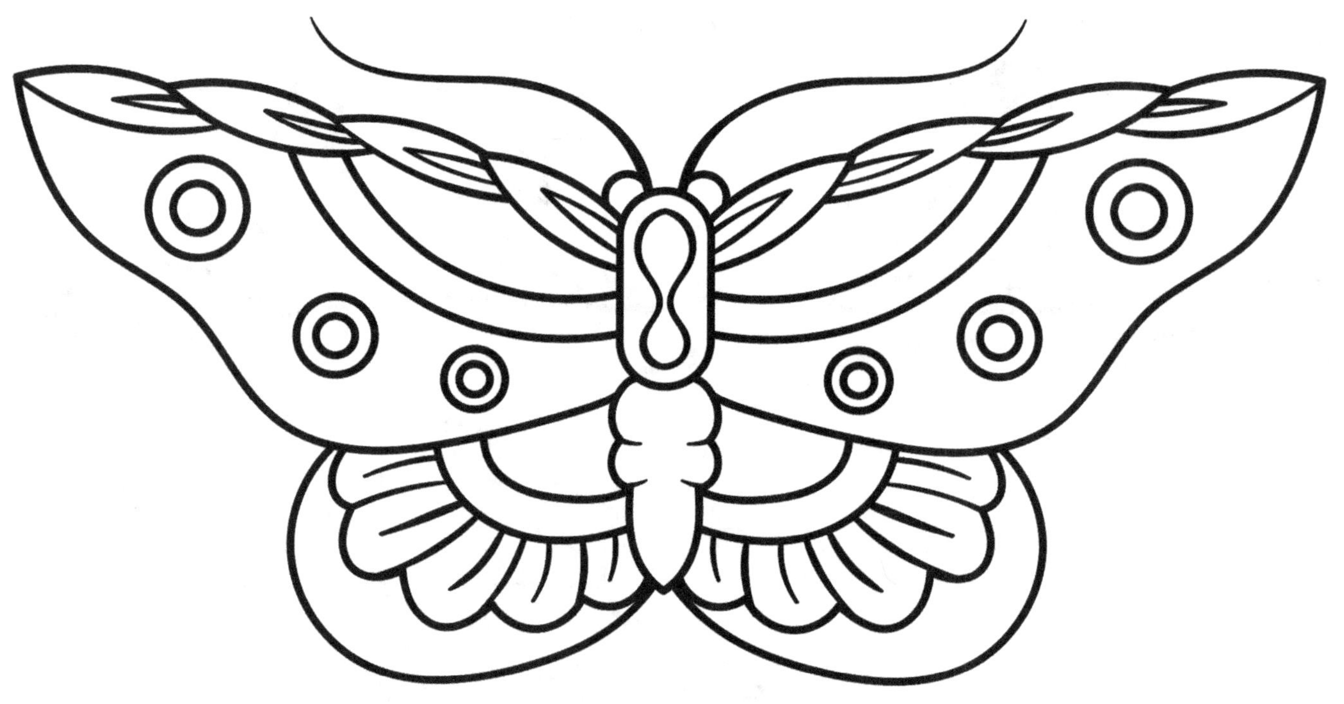

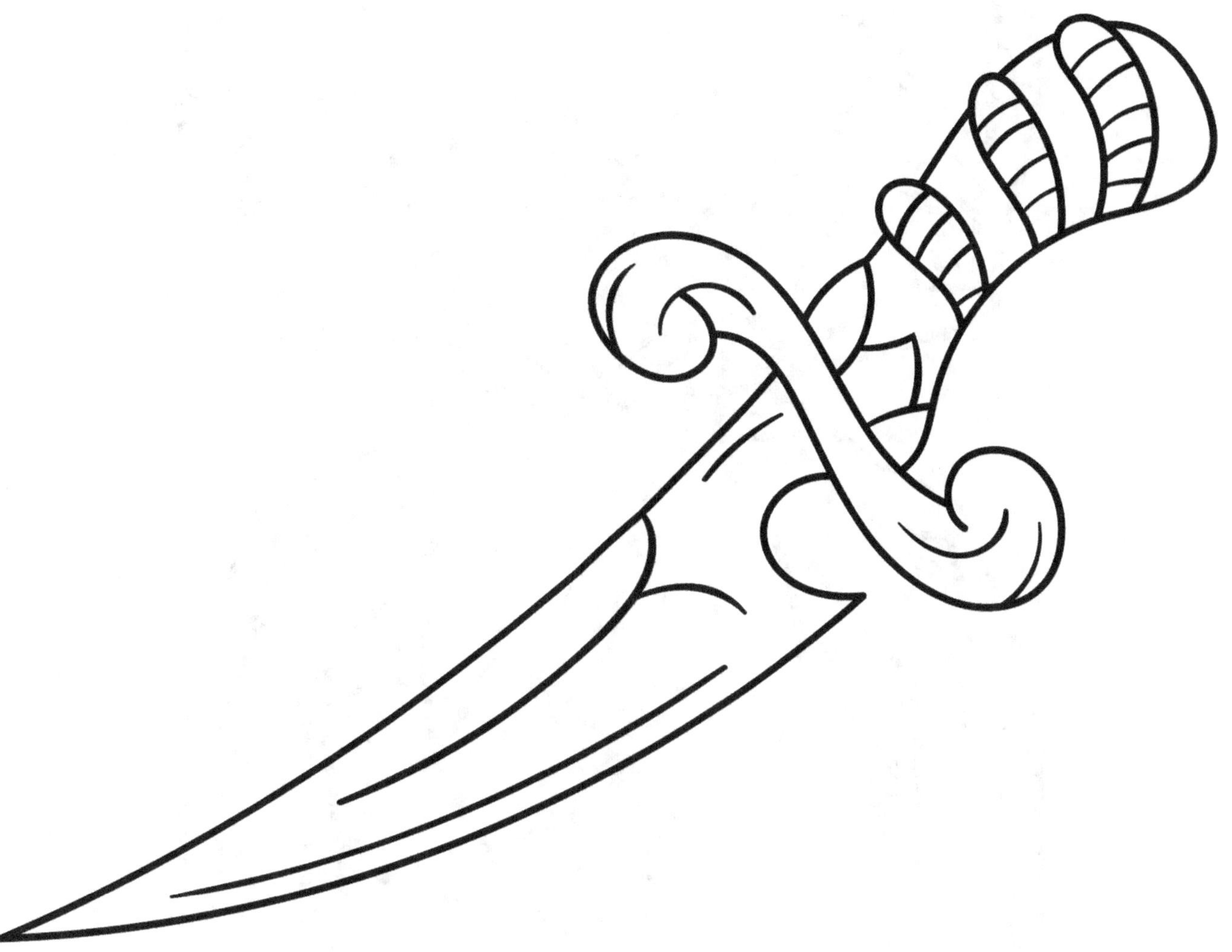

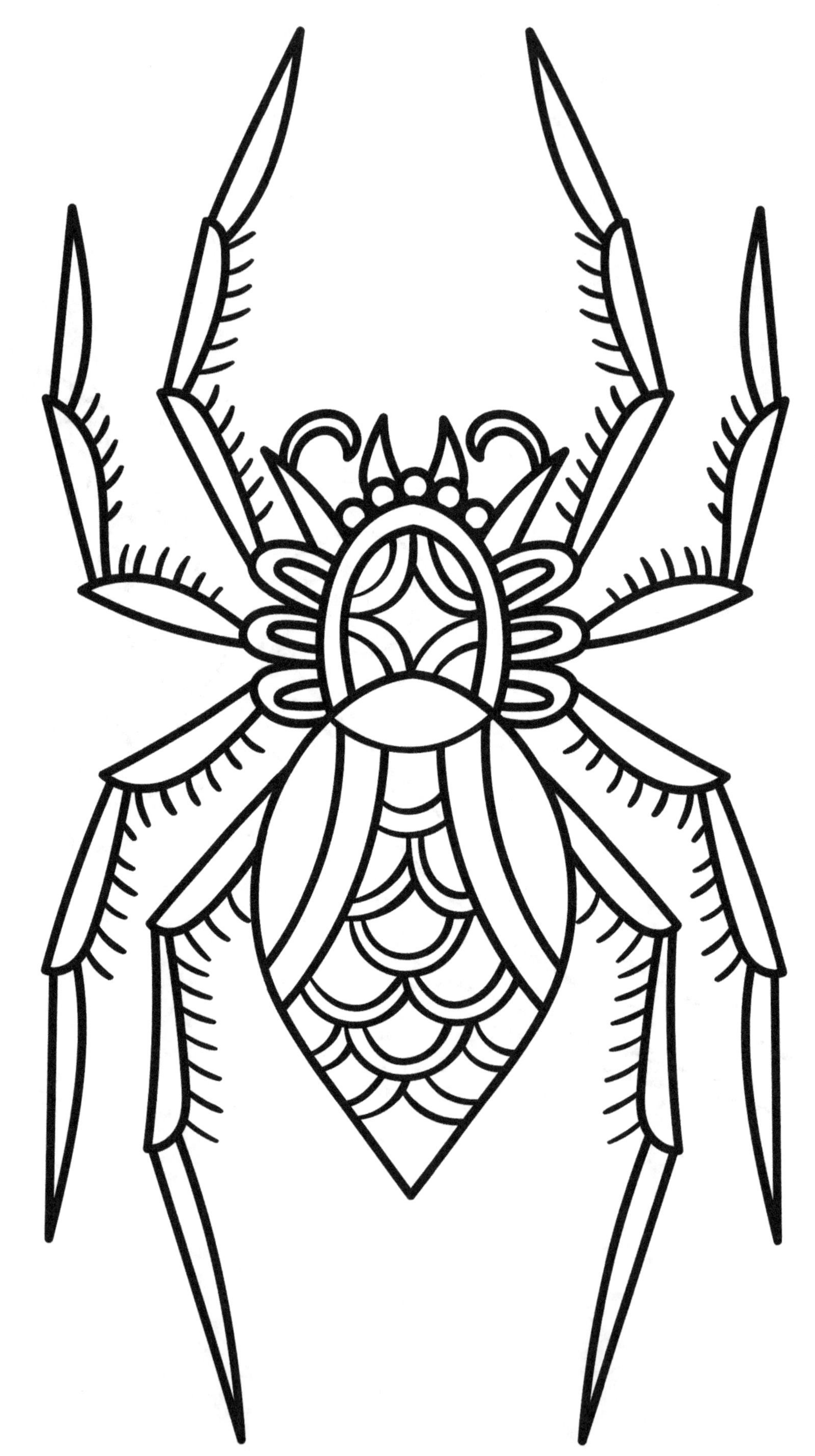

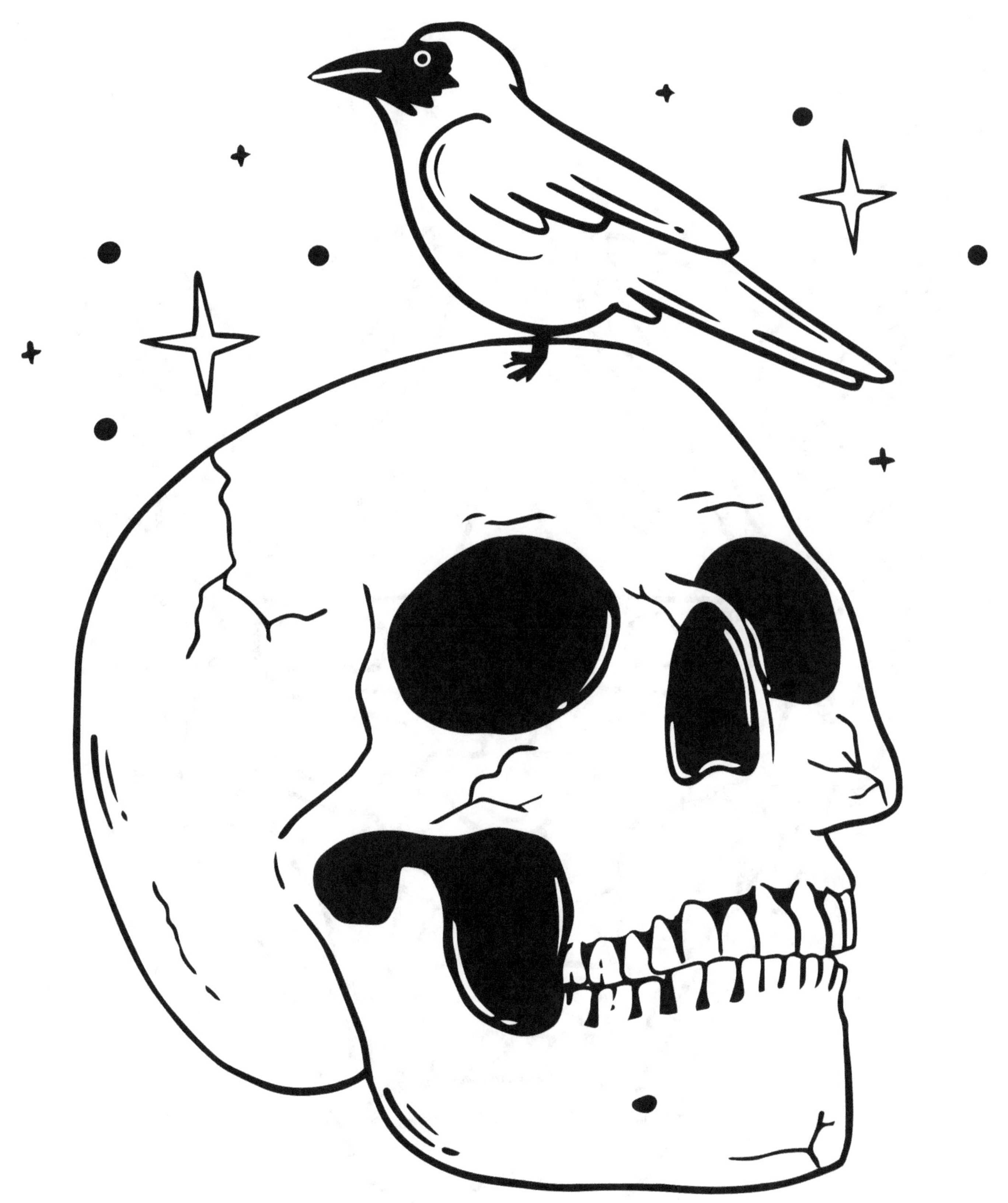

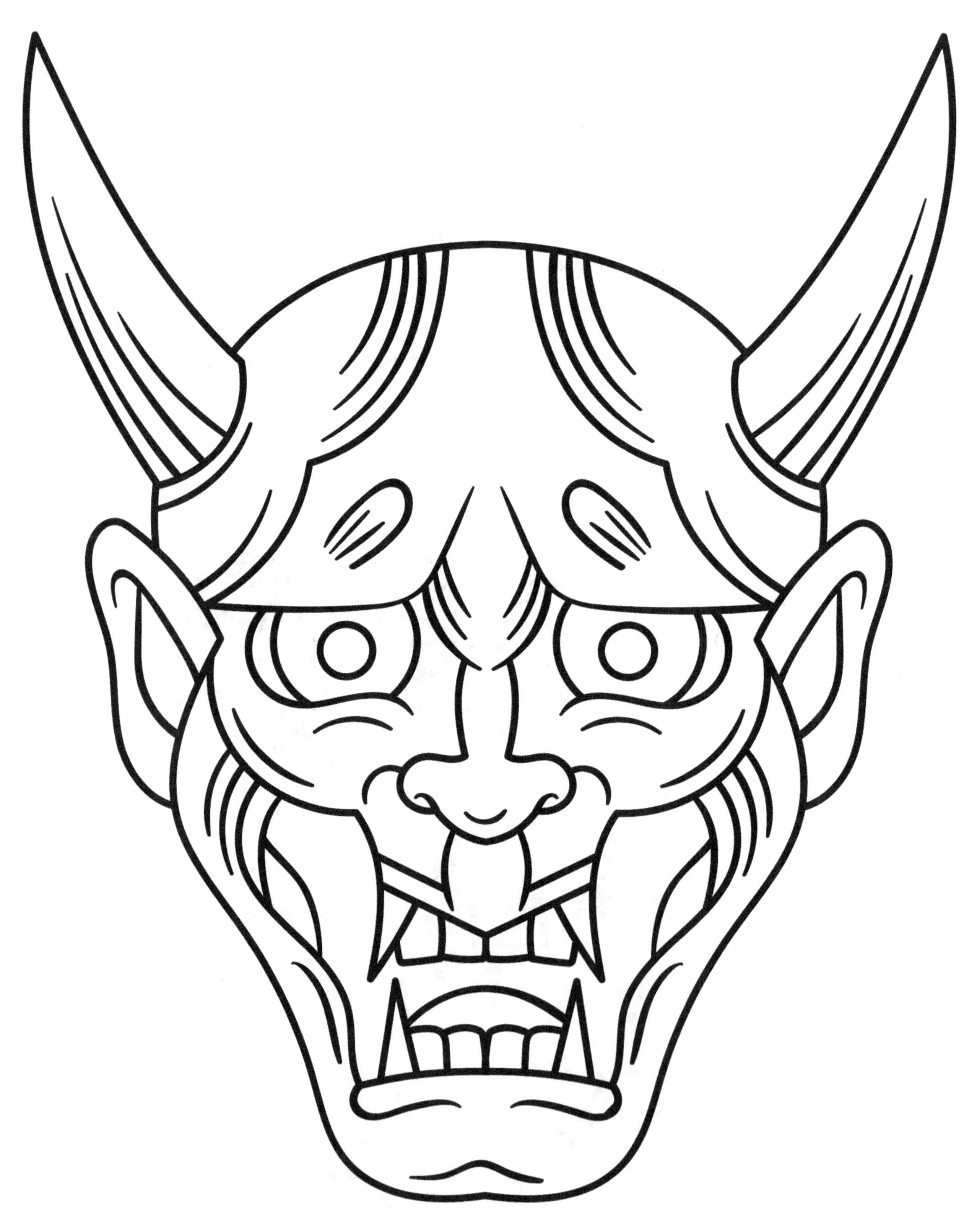

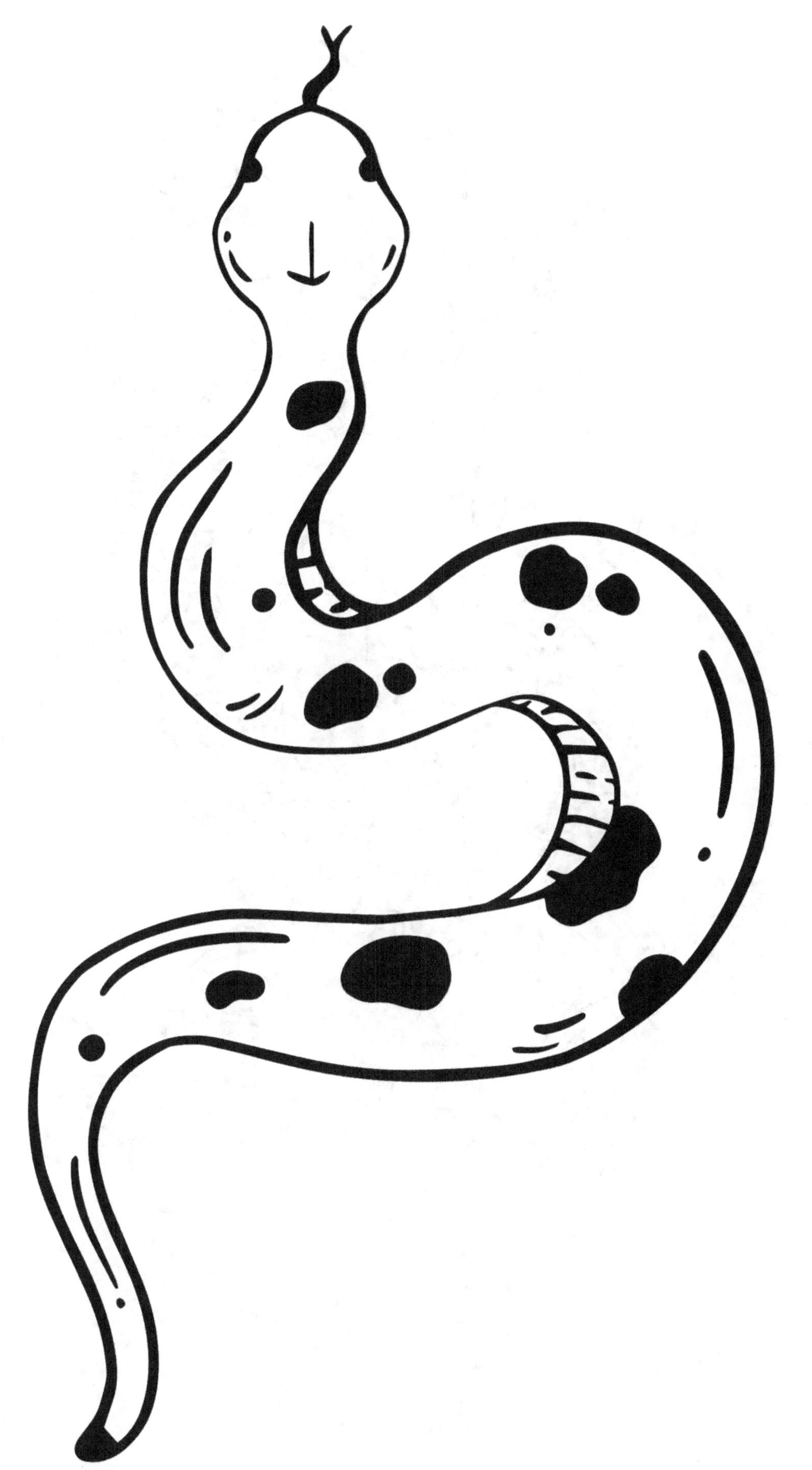

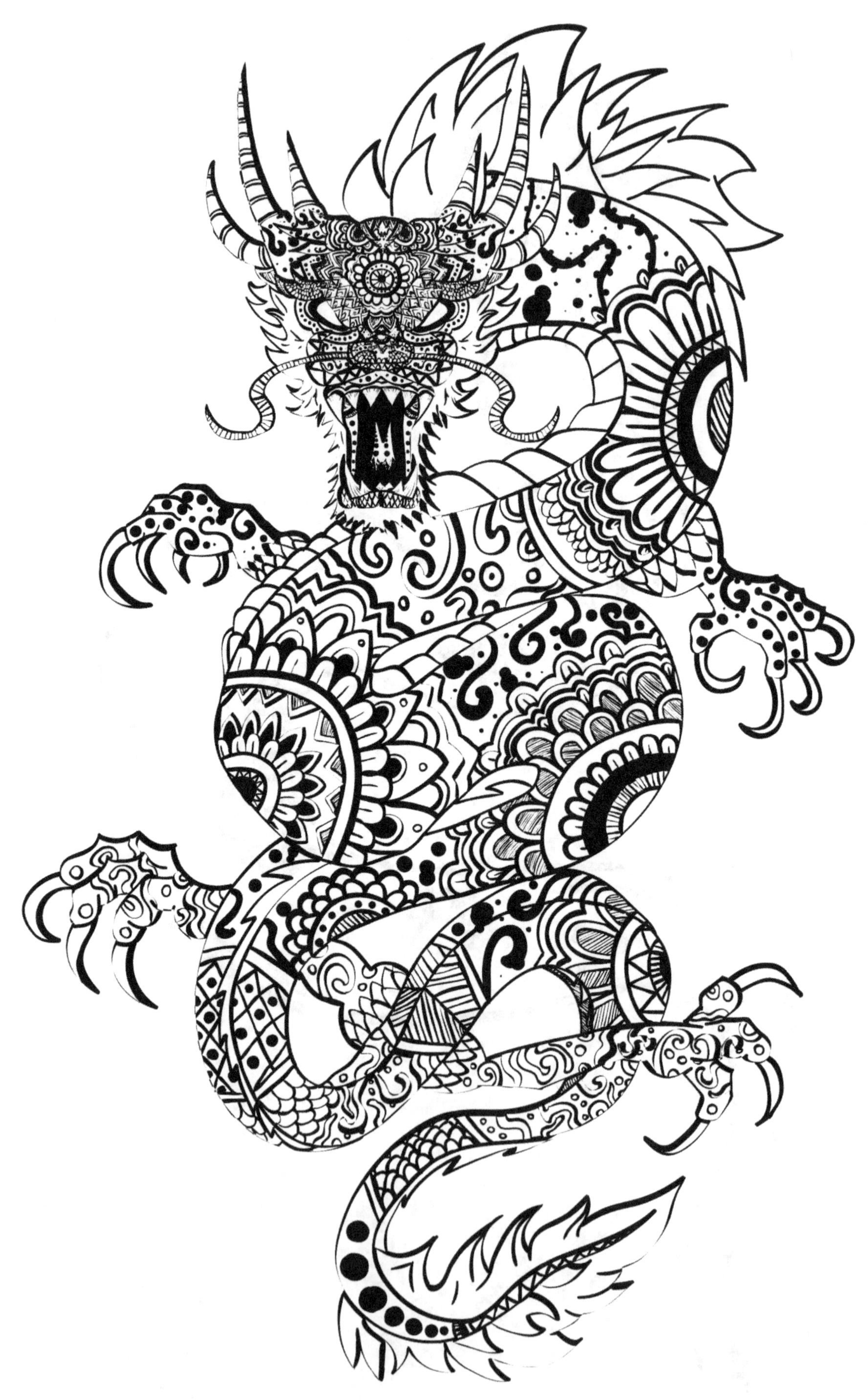

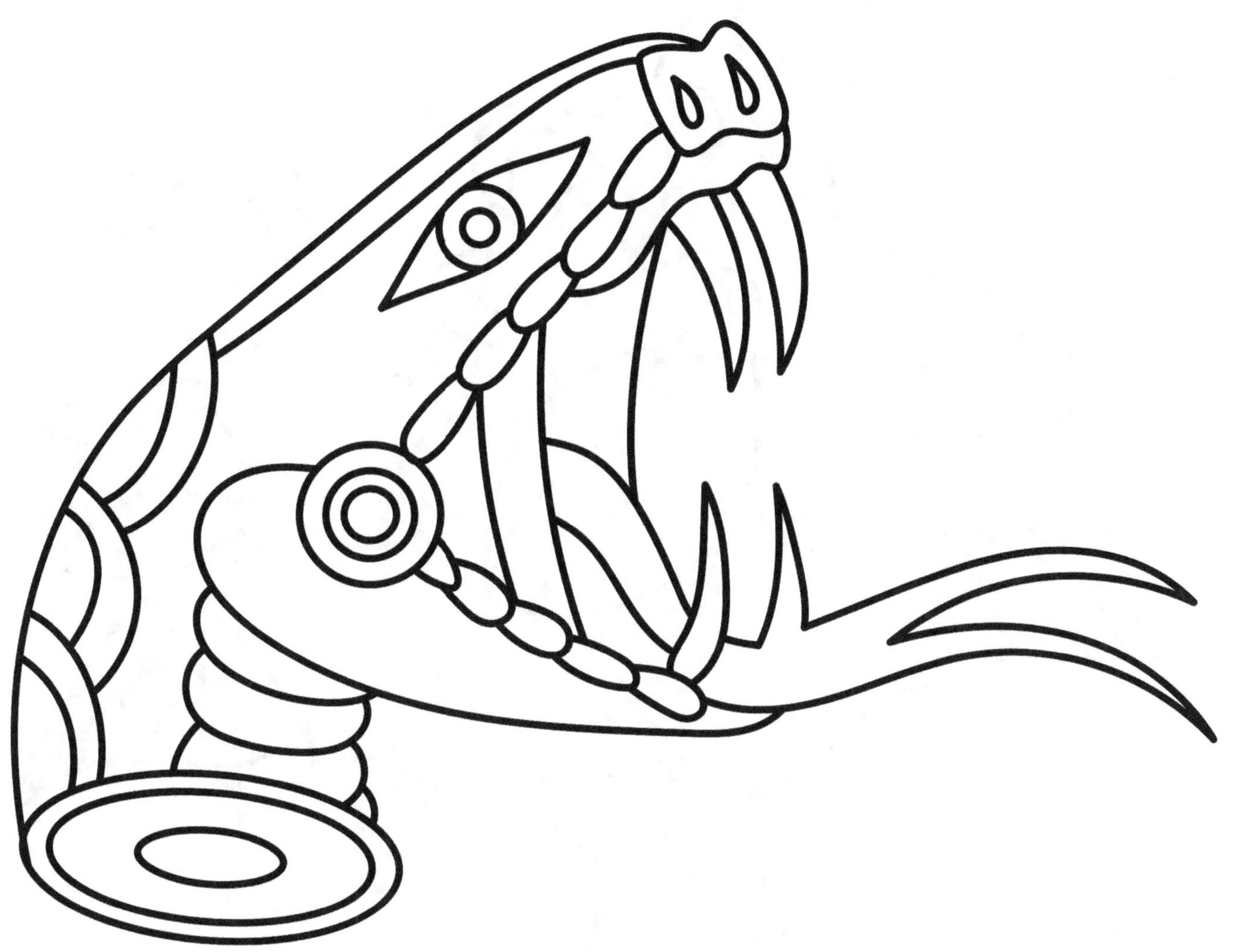

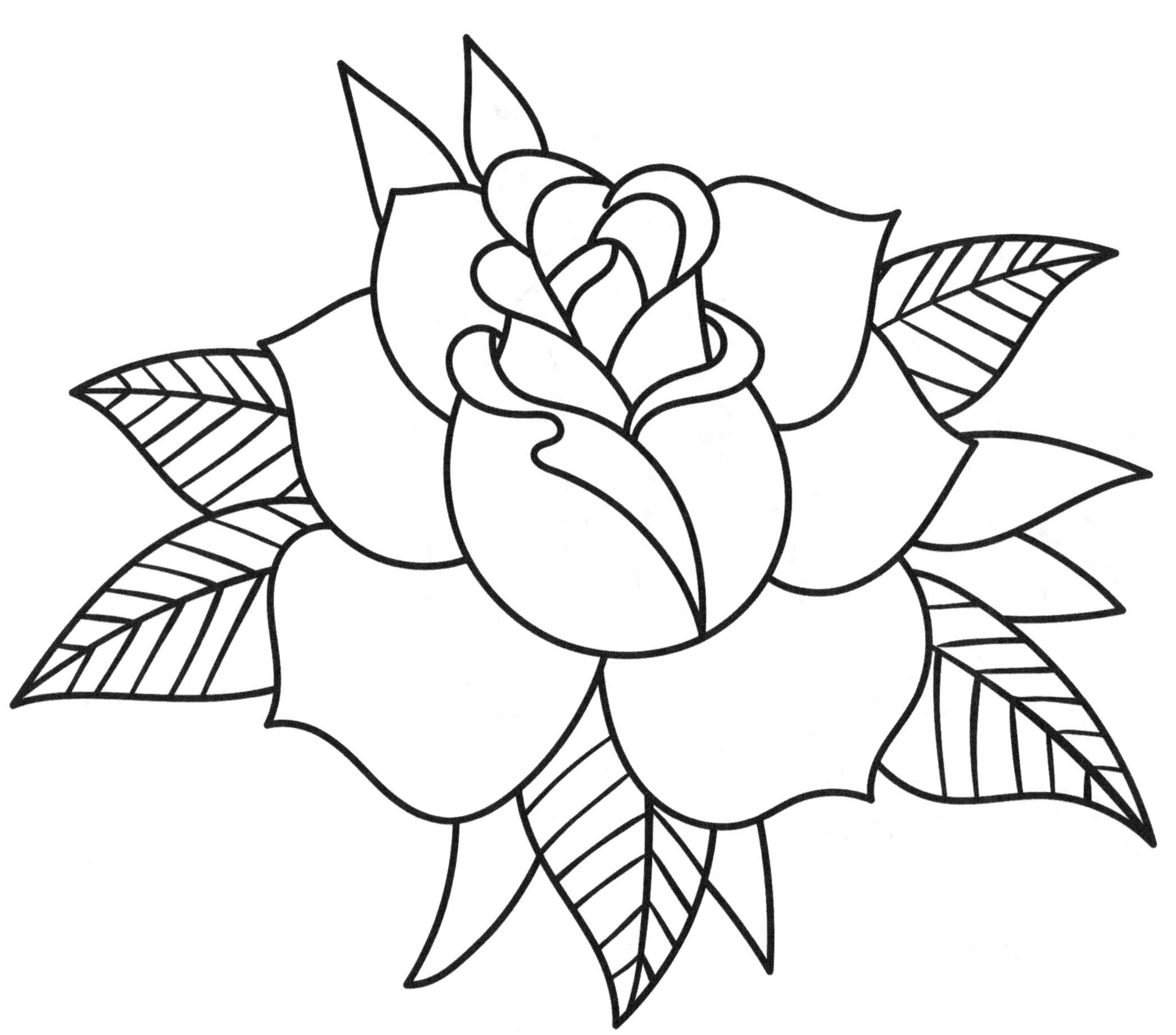

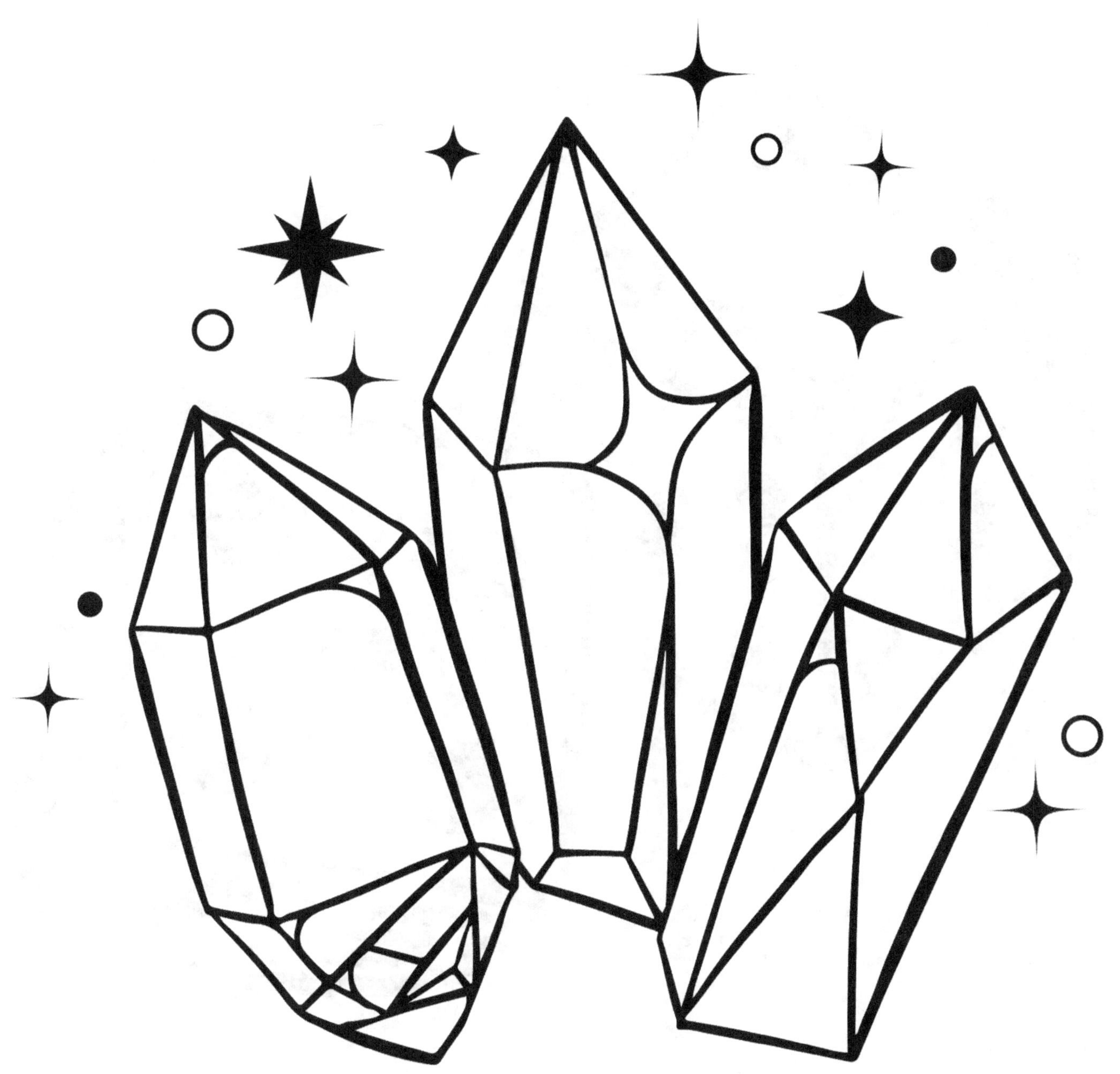

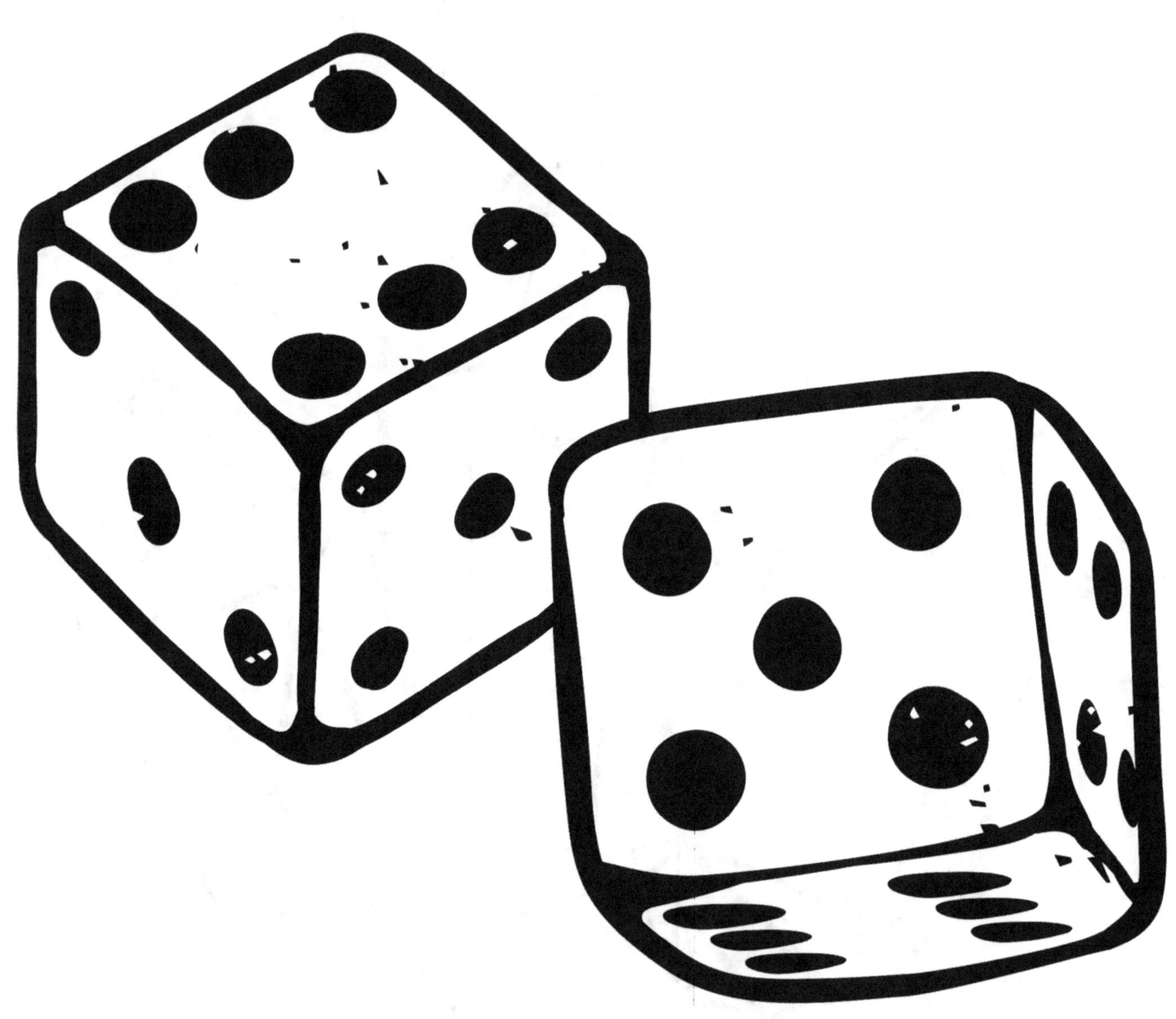

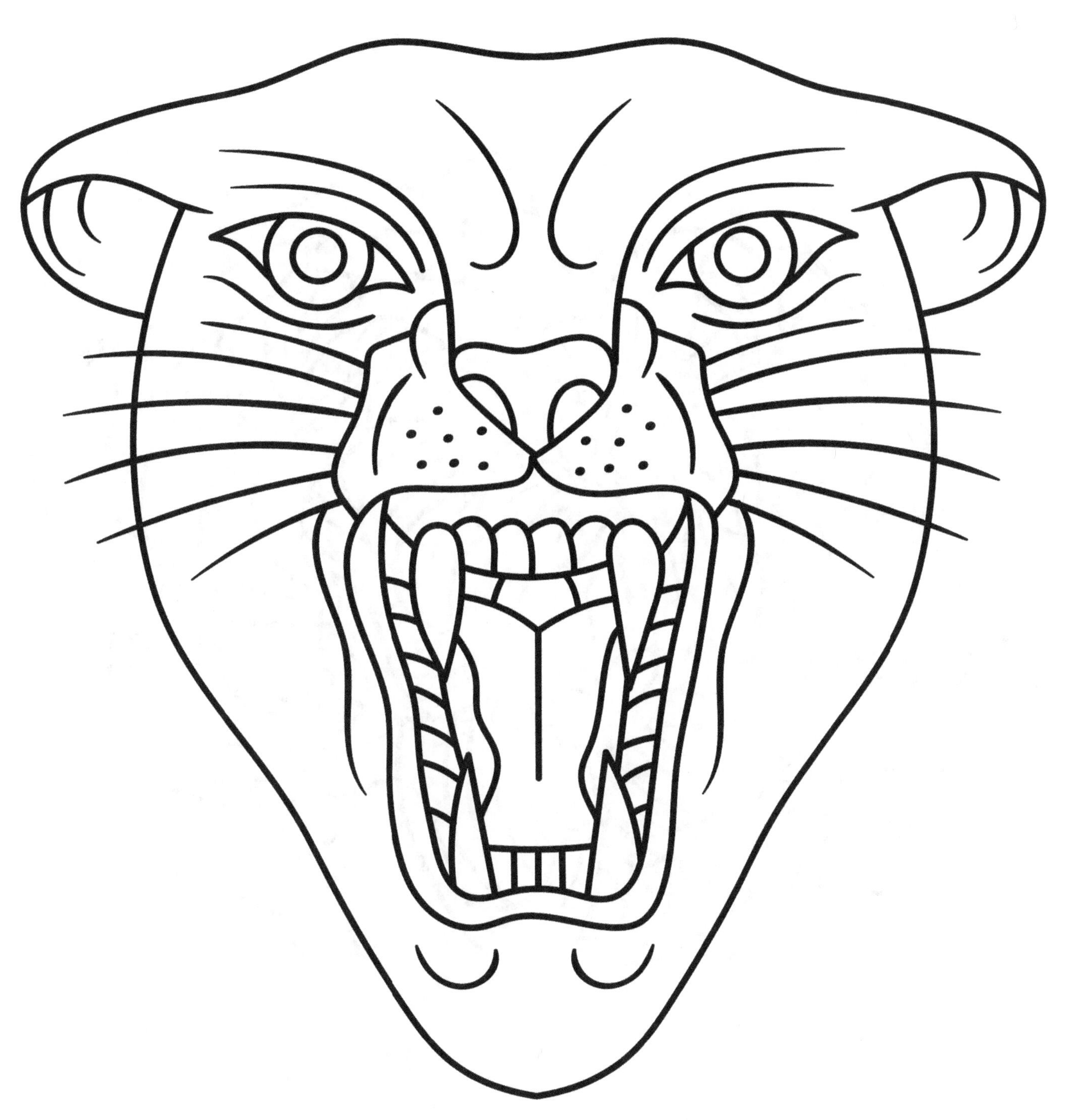

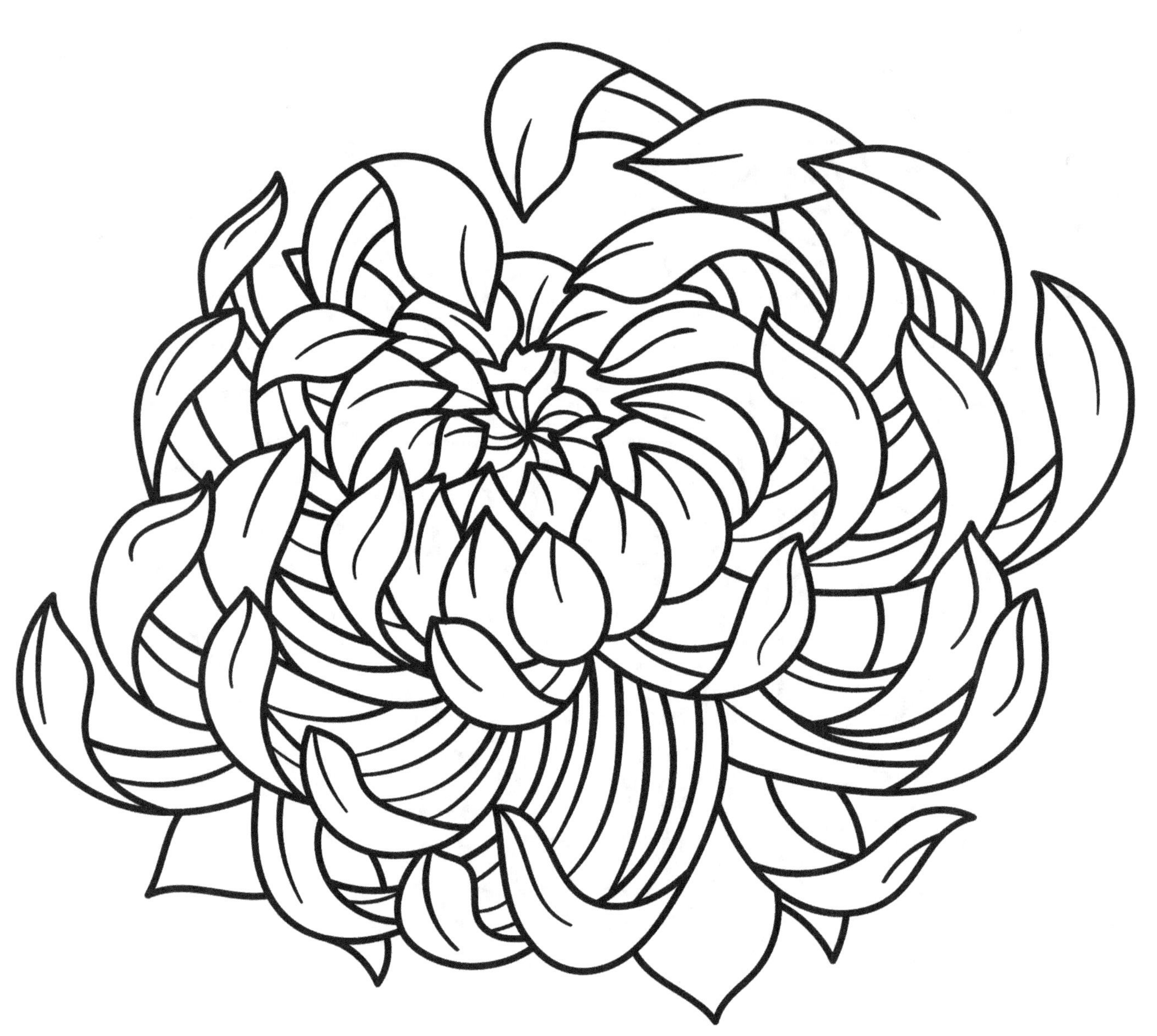

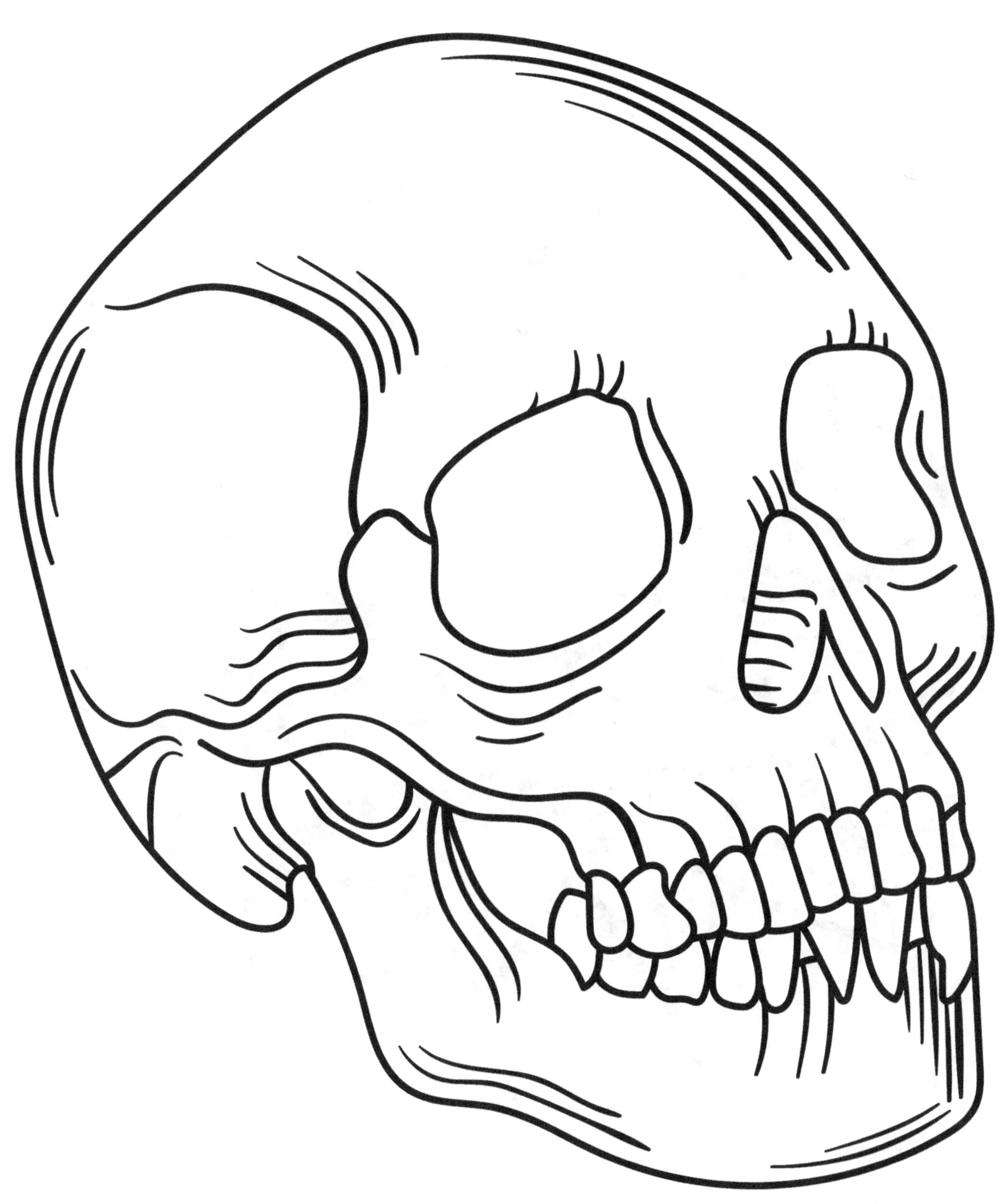

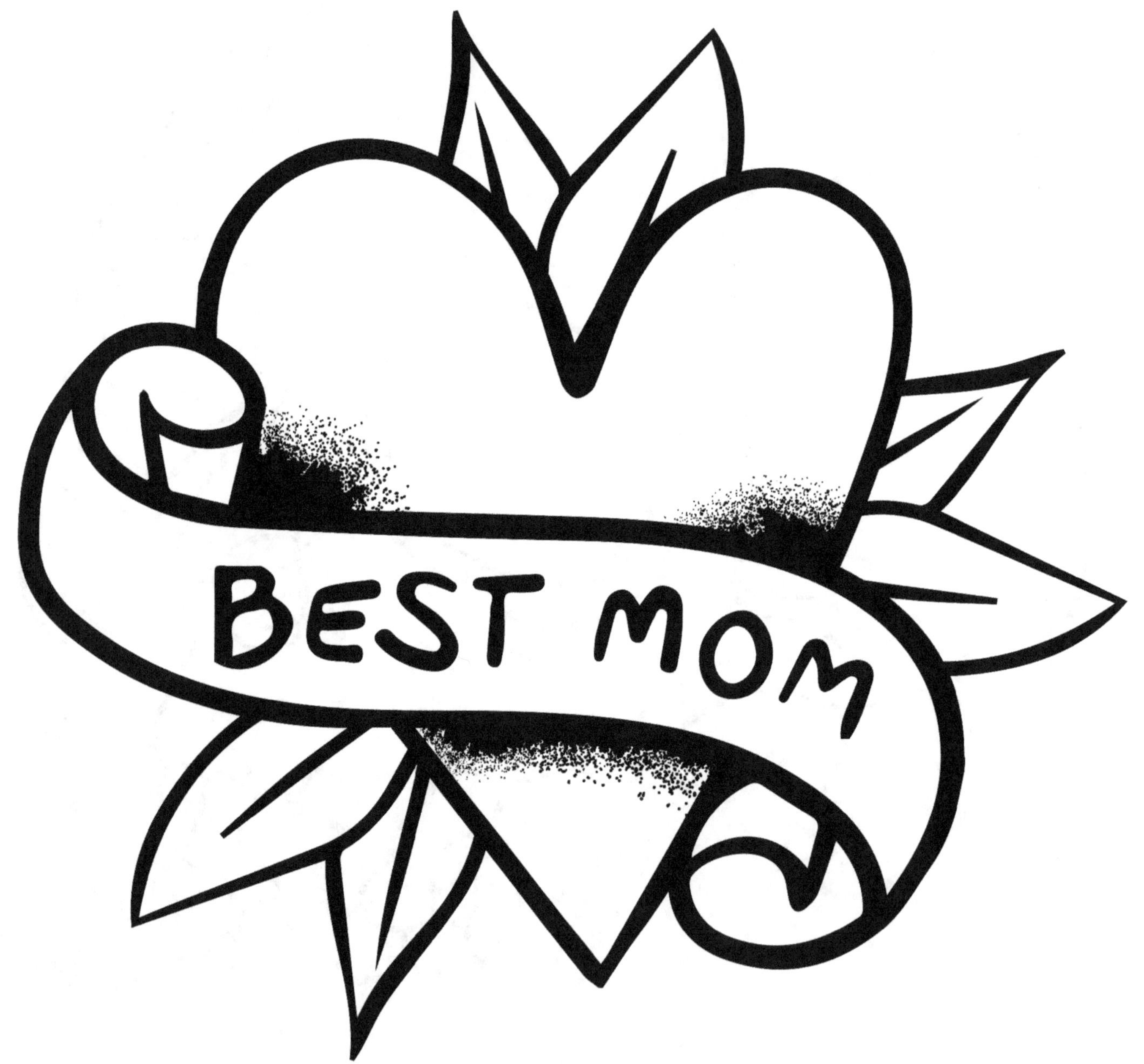

BEST MOM

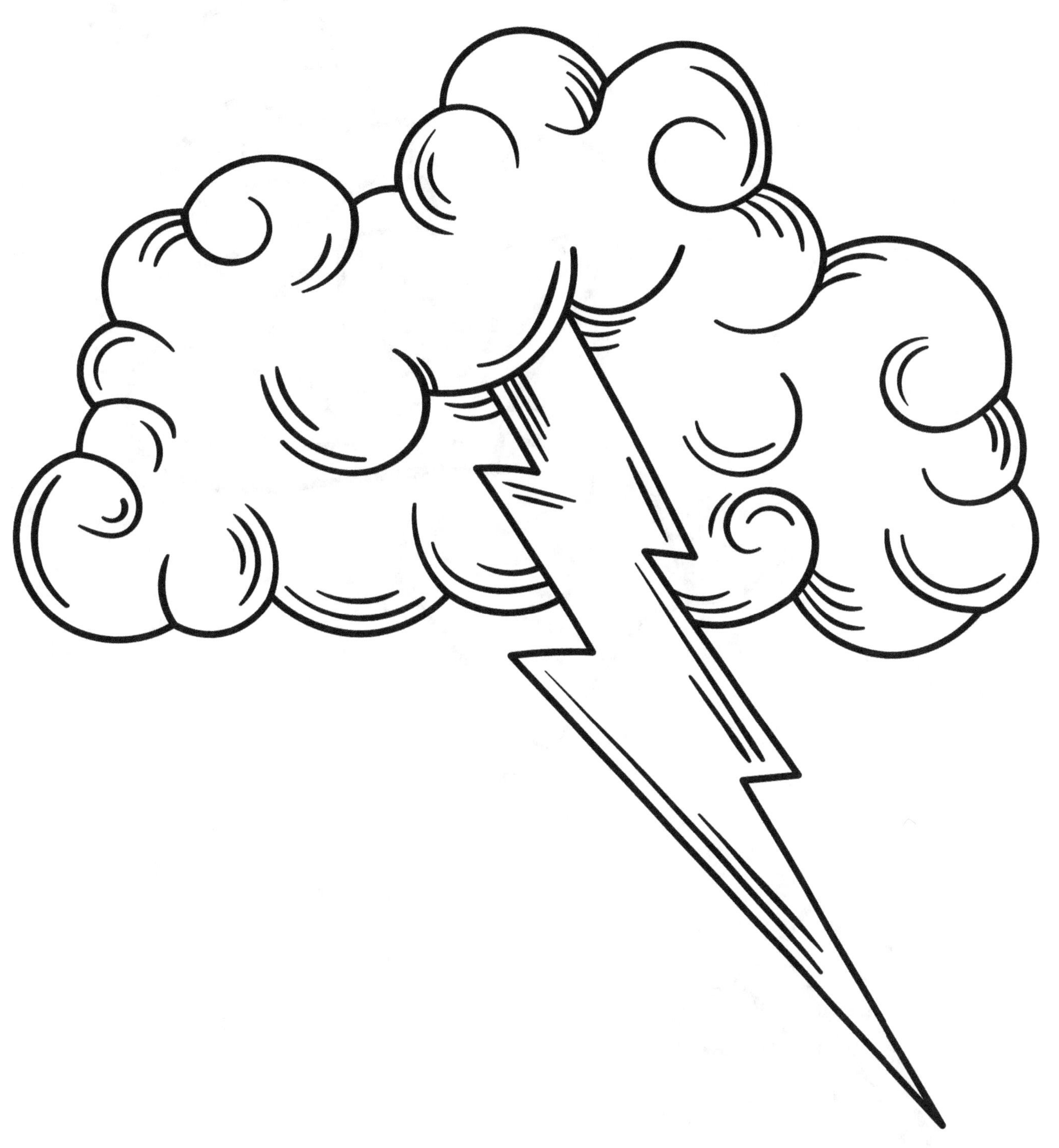

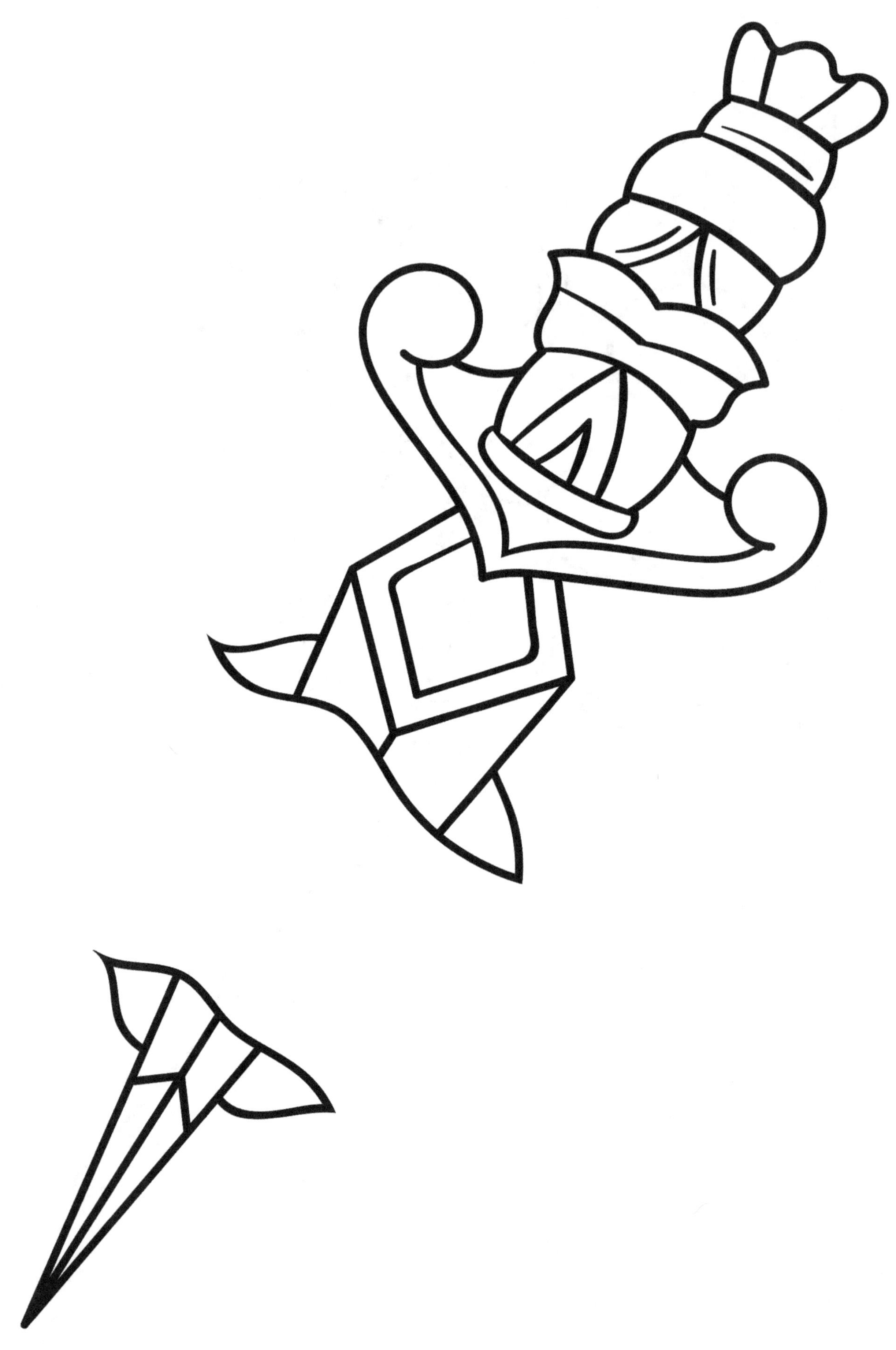

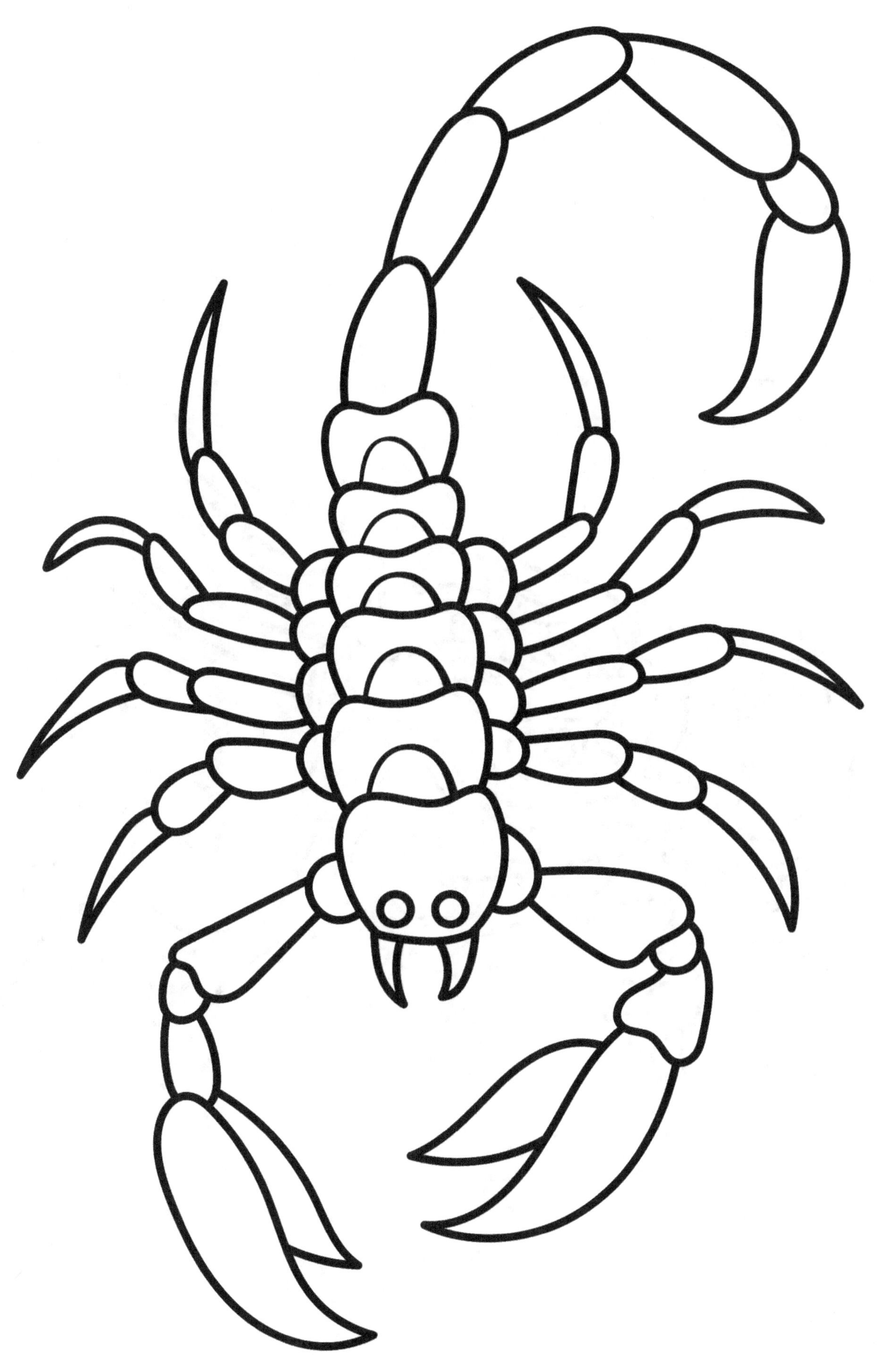

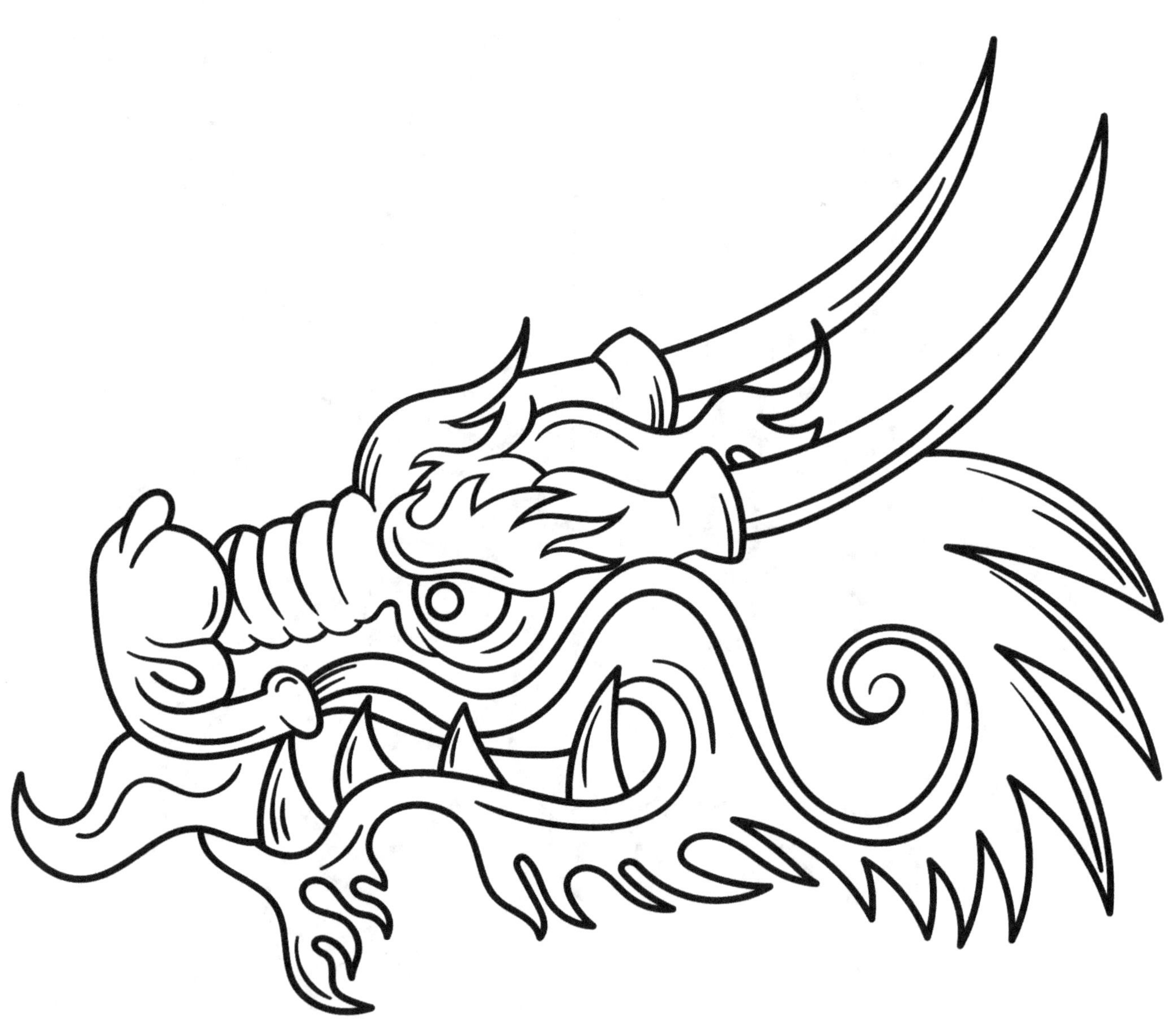

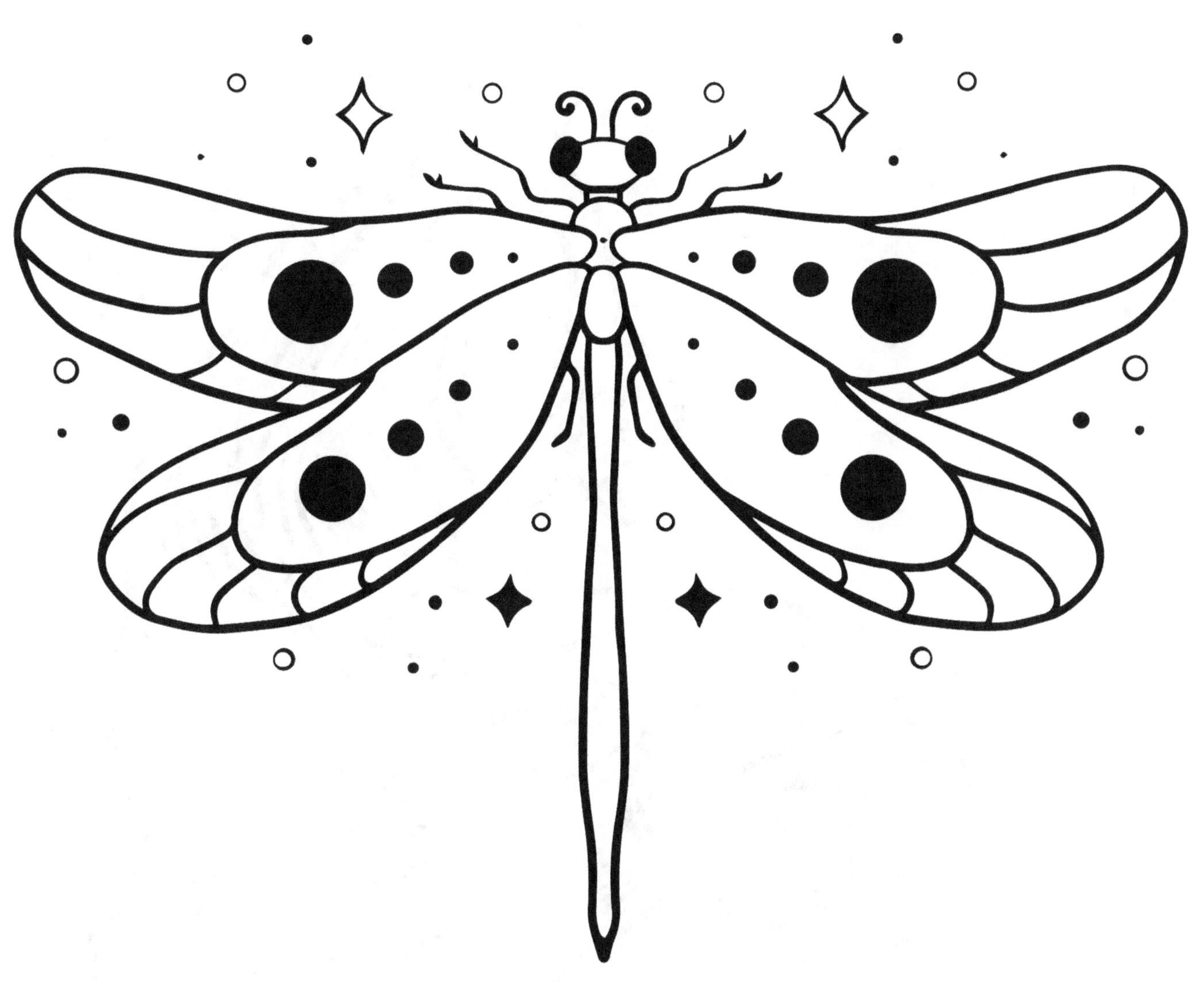

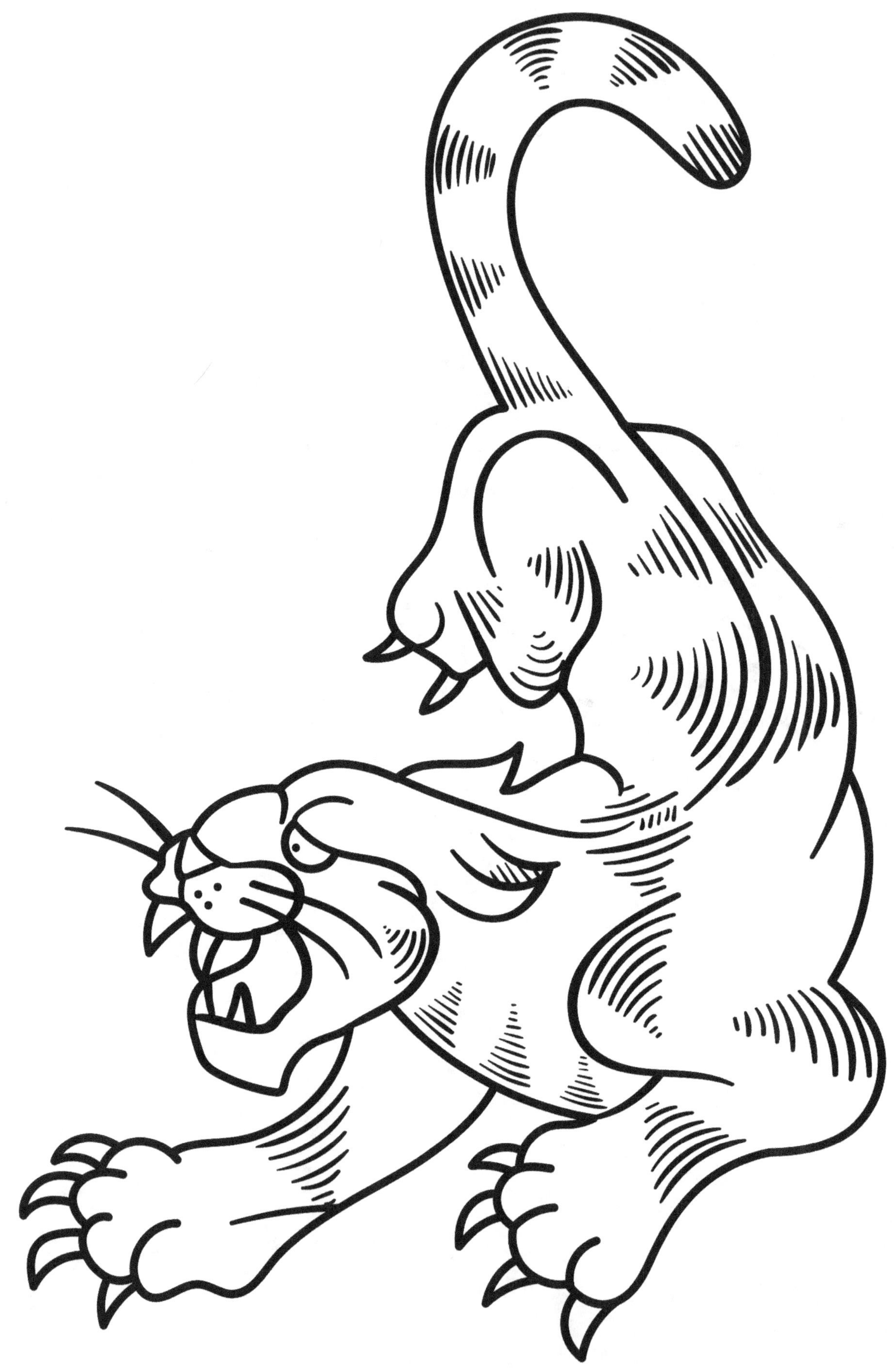

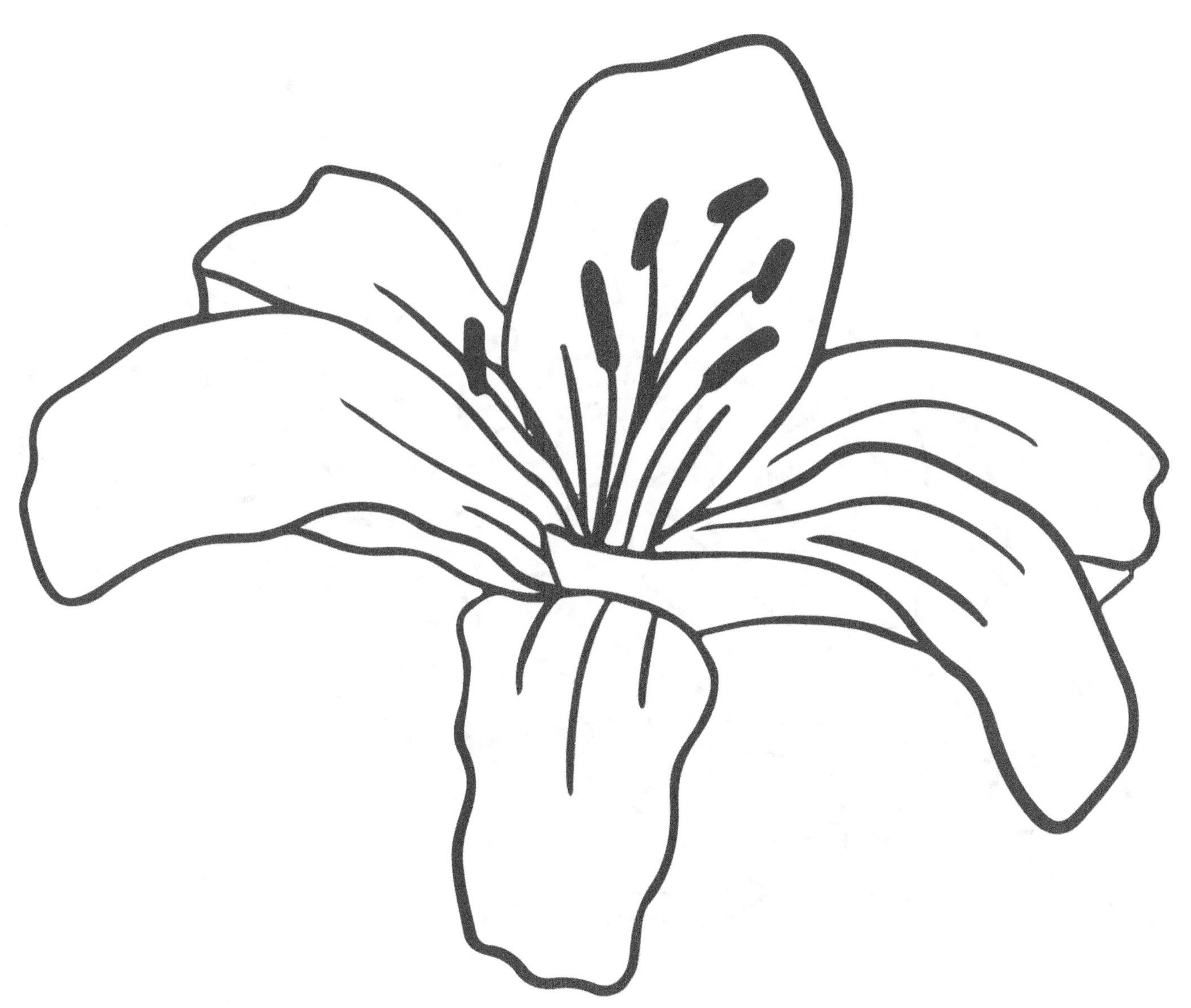

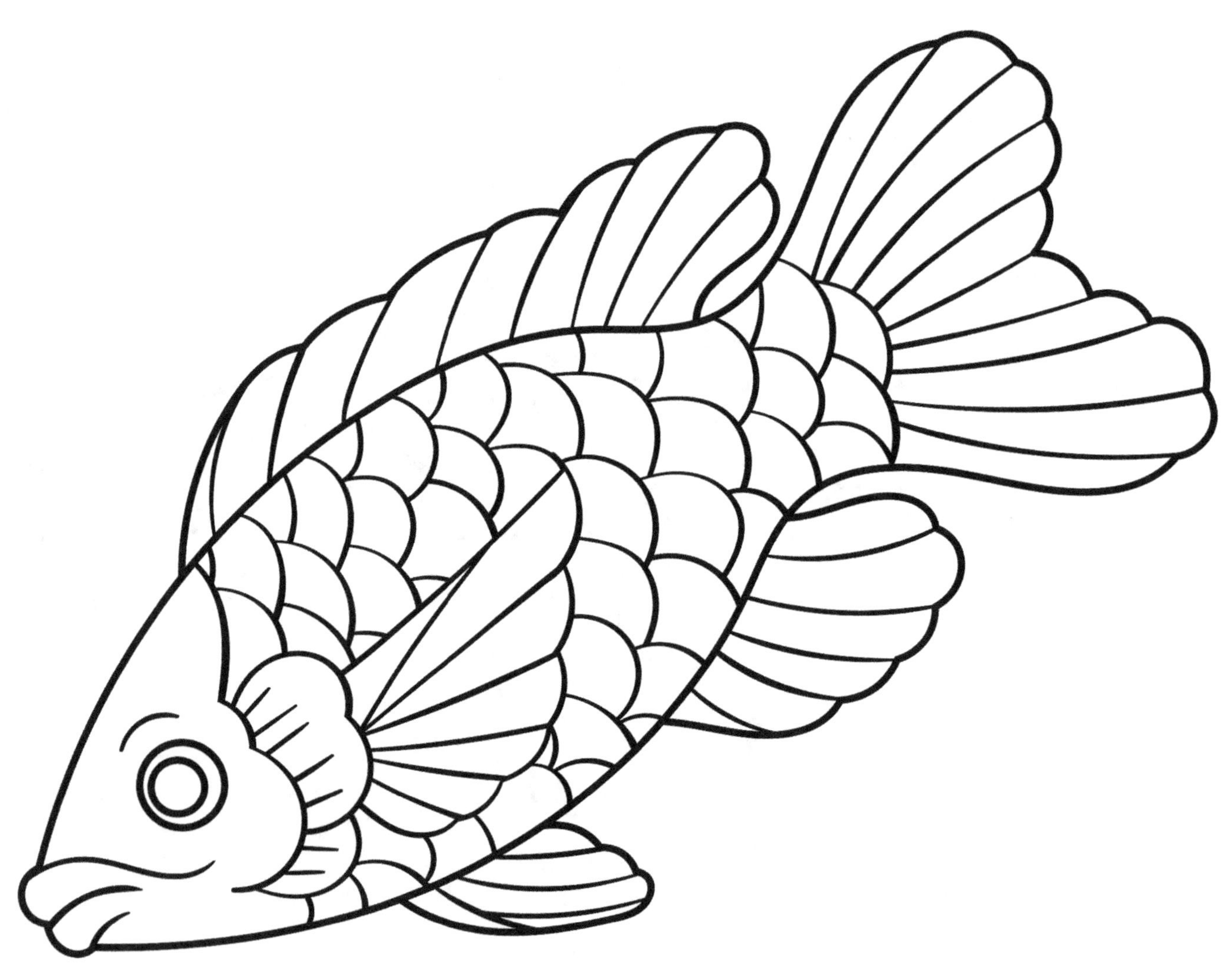

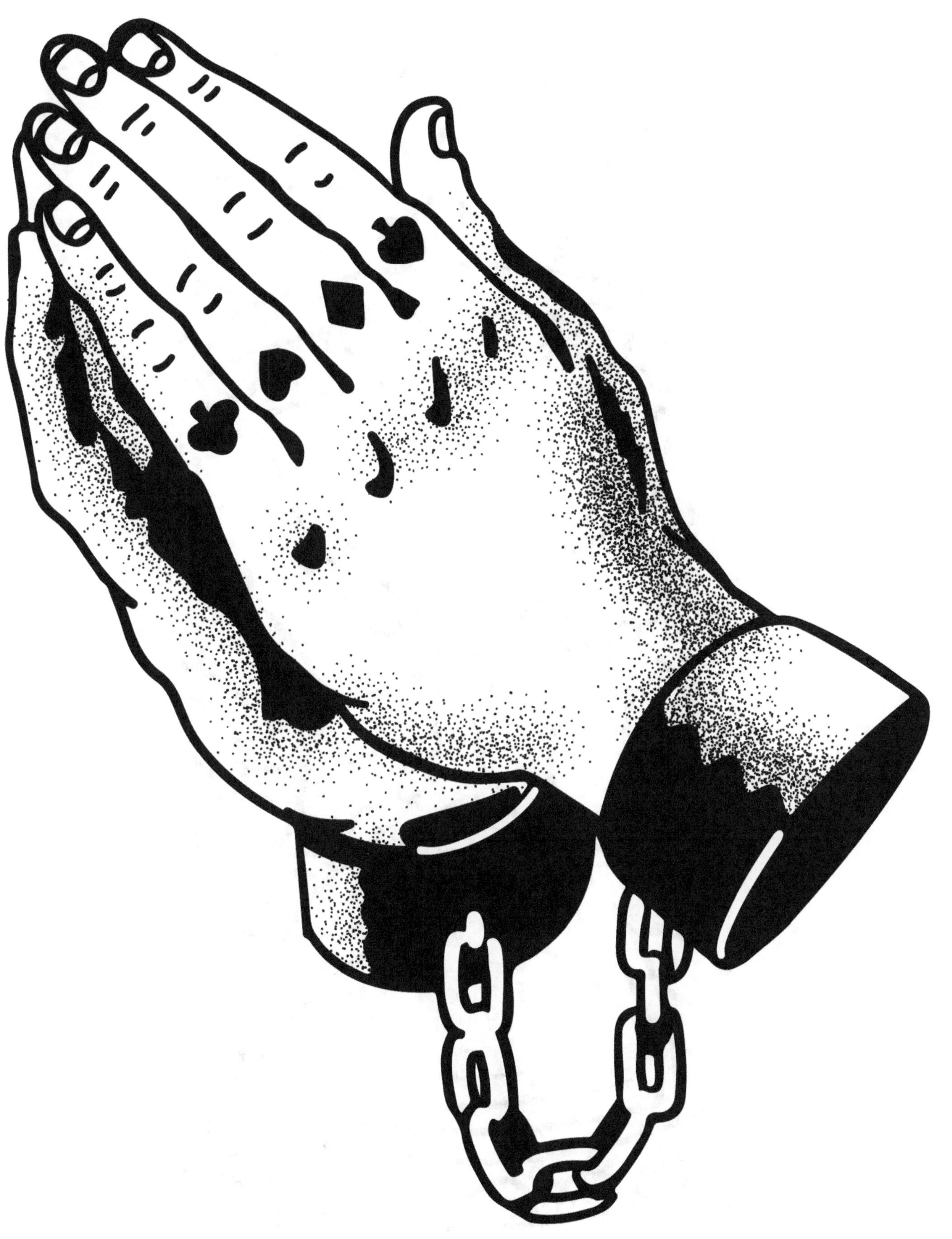

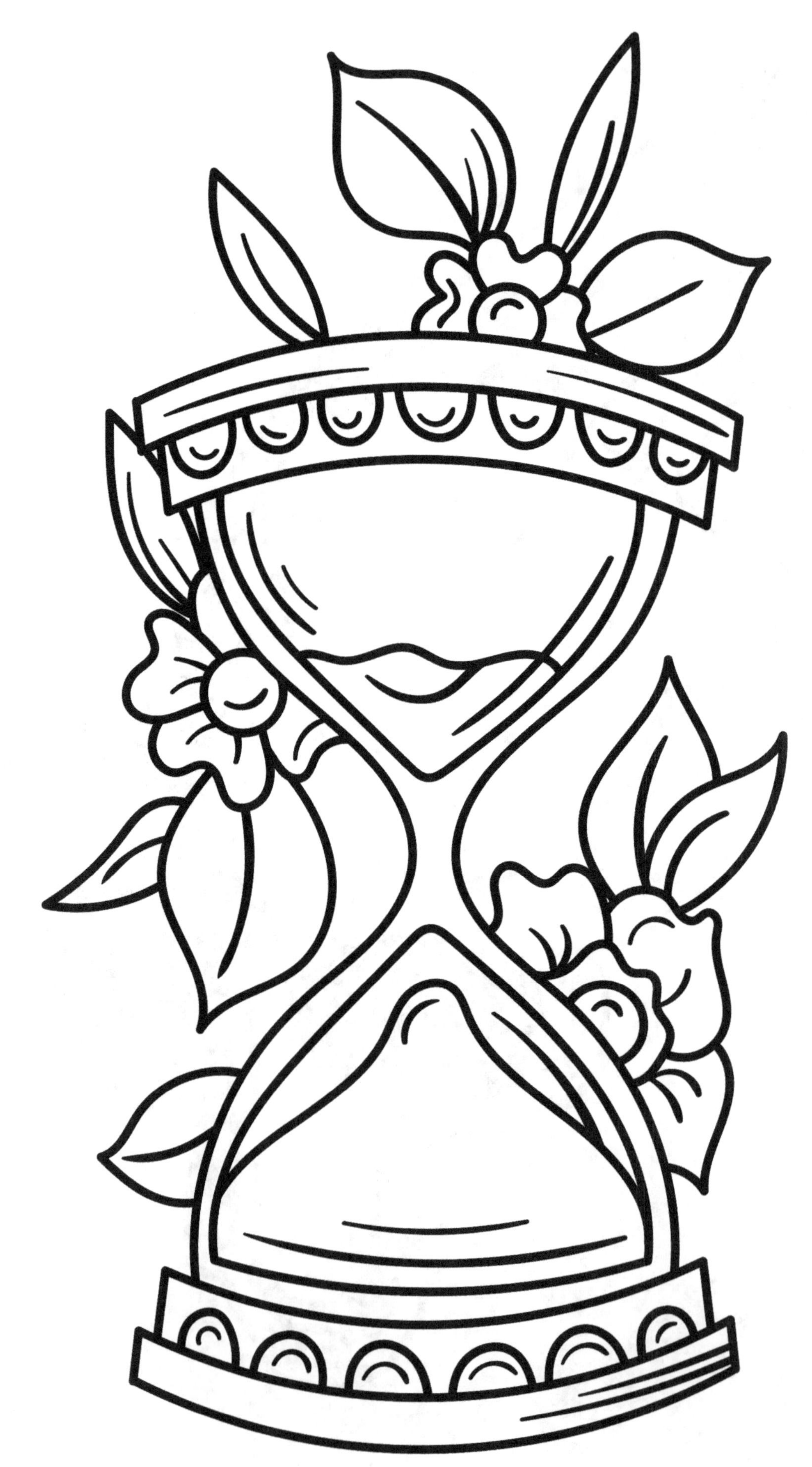

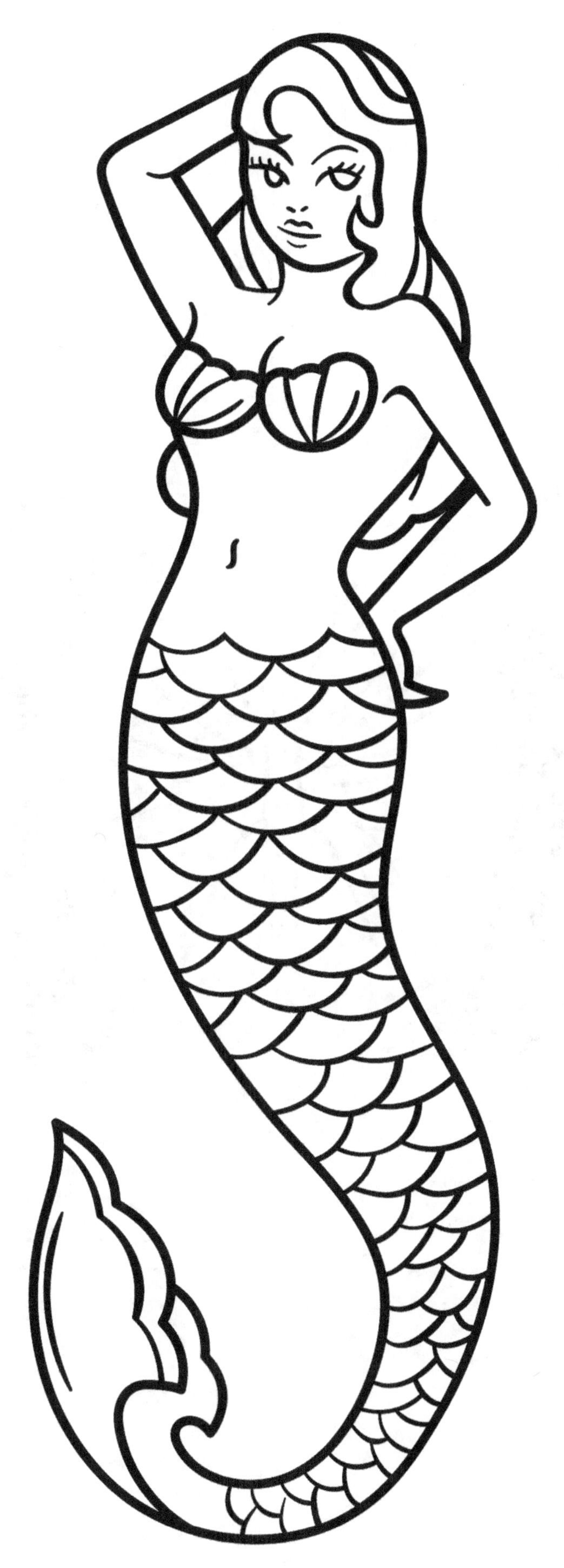

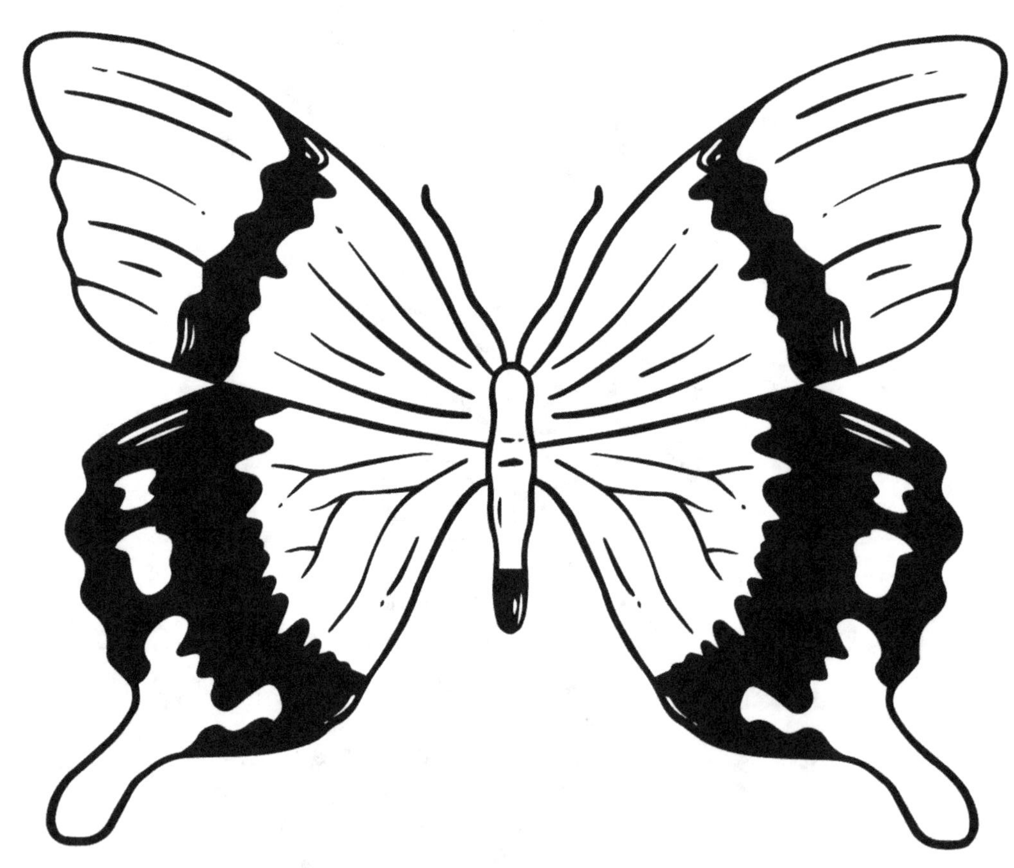

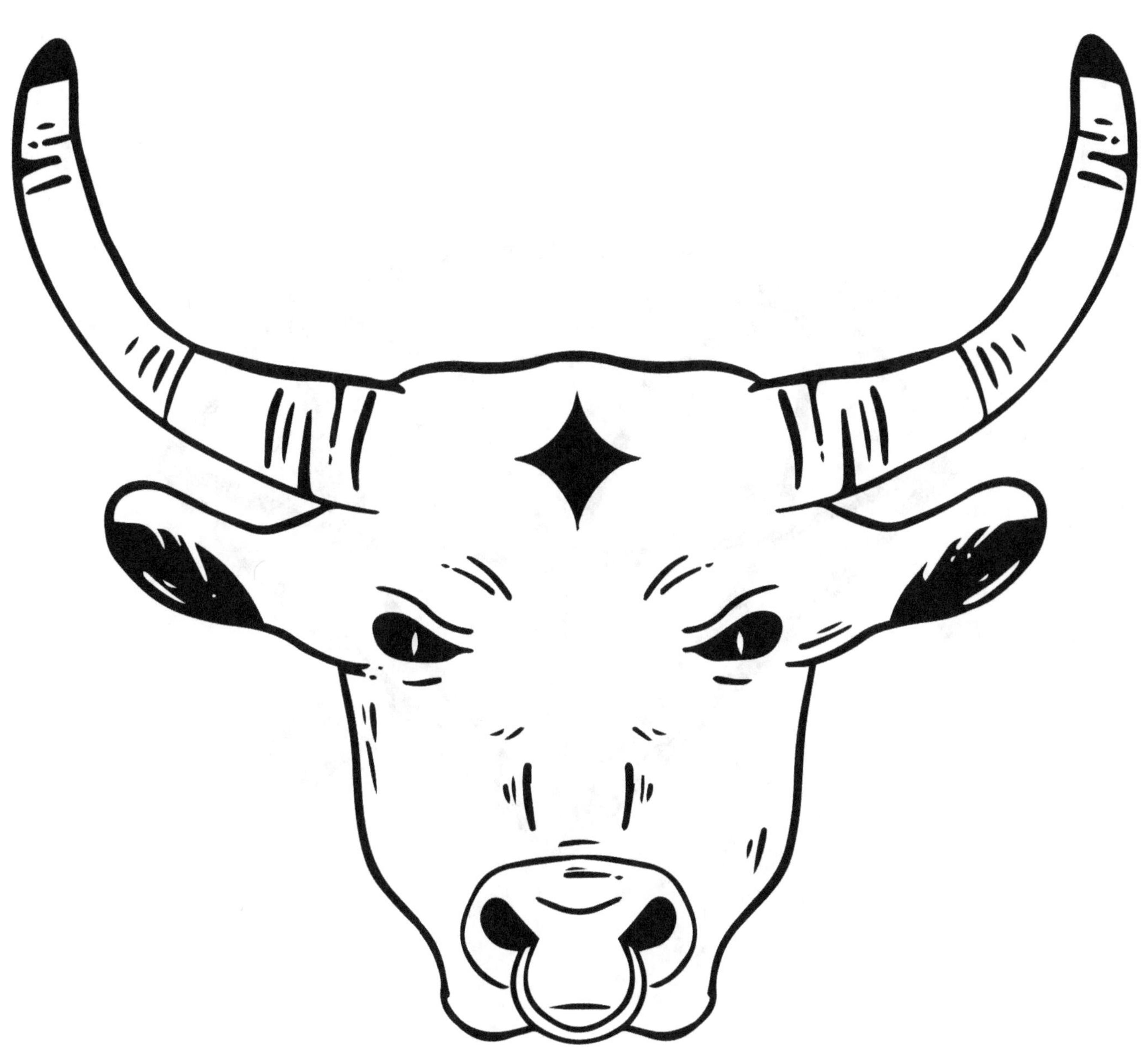

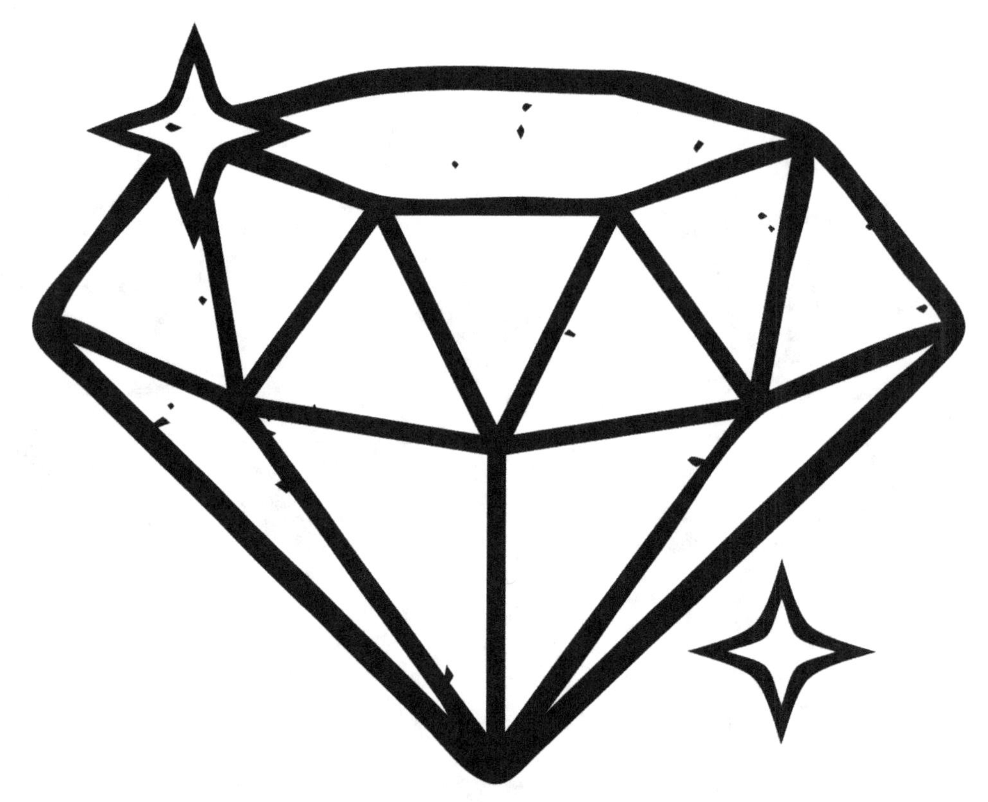

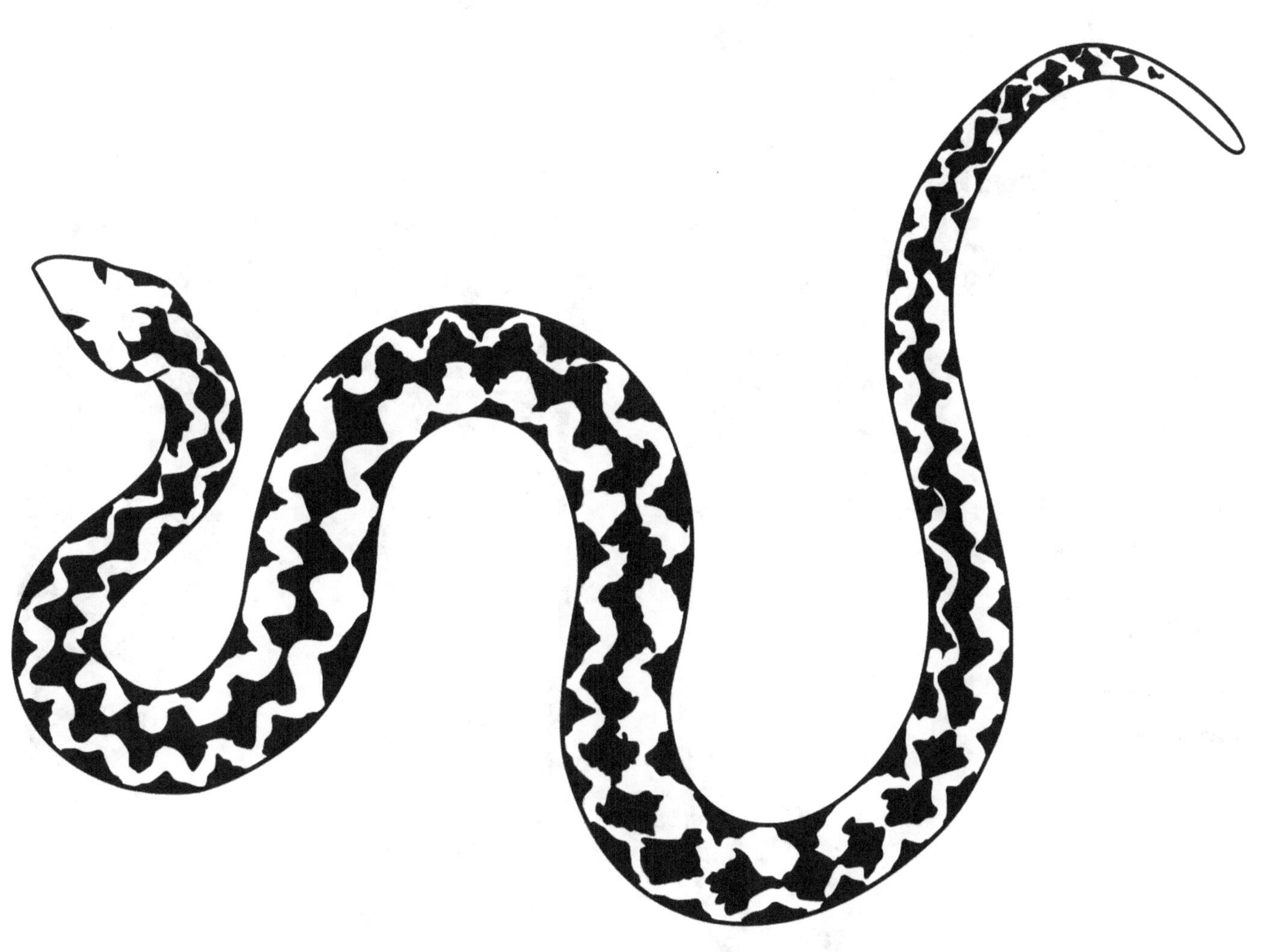

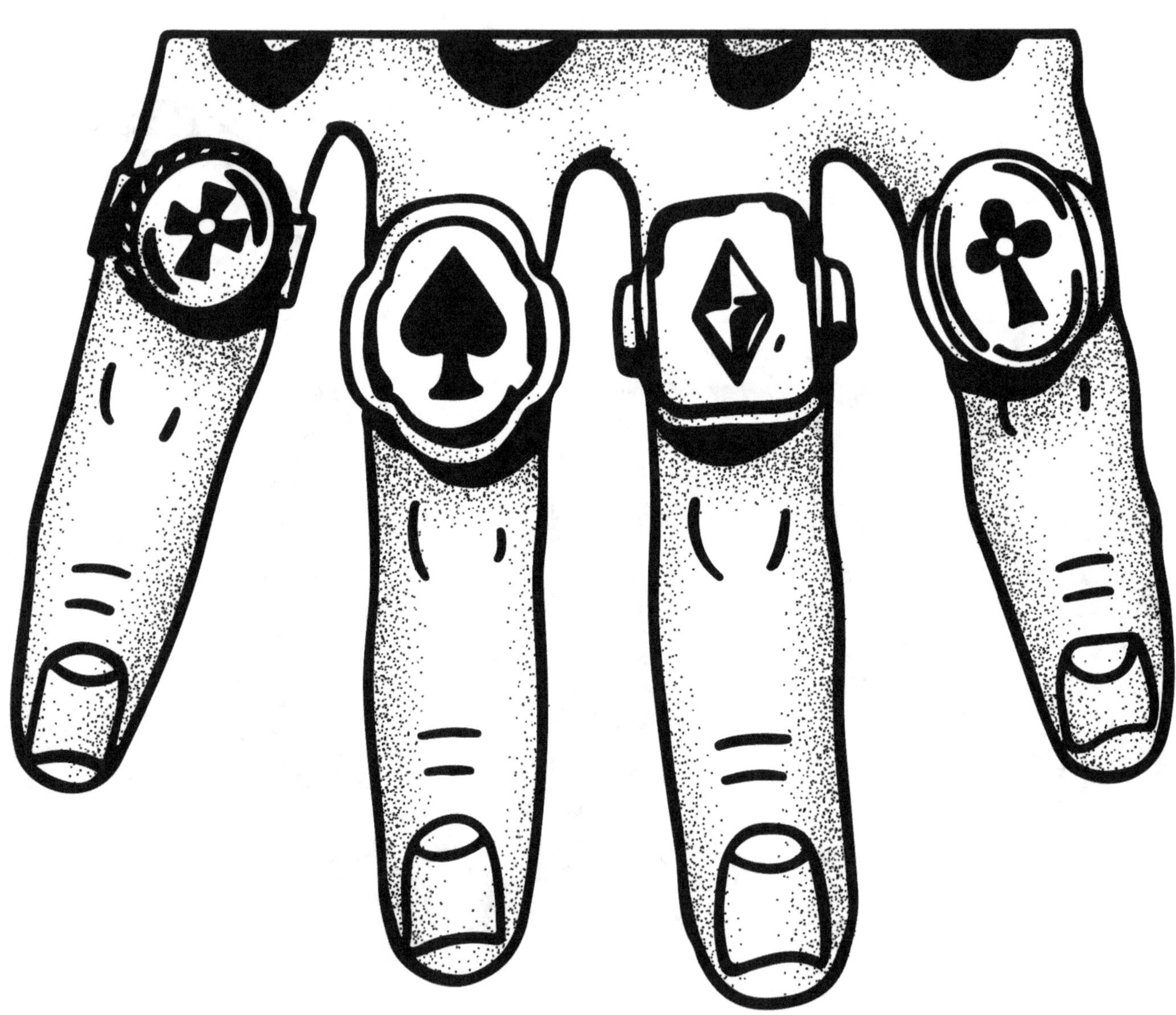

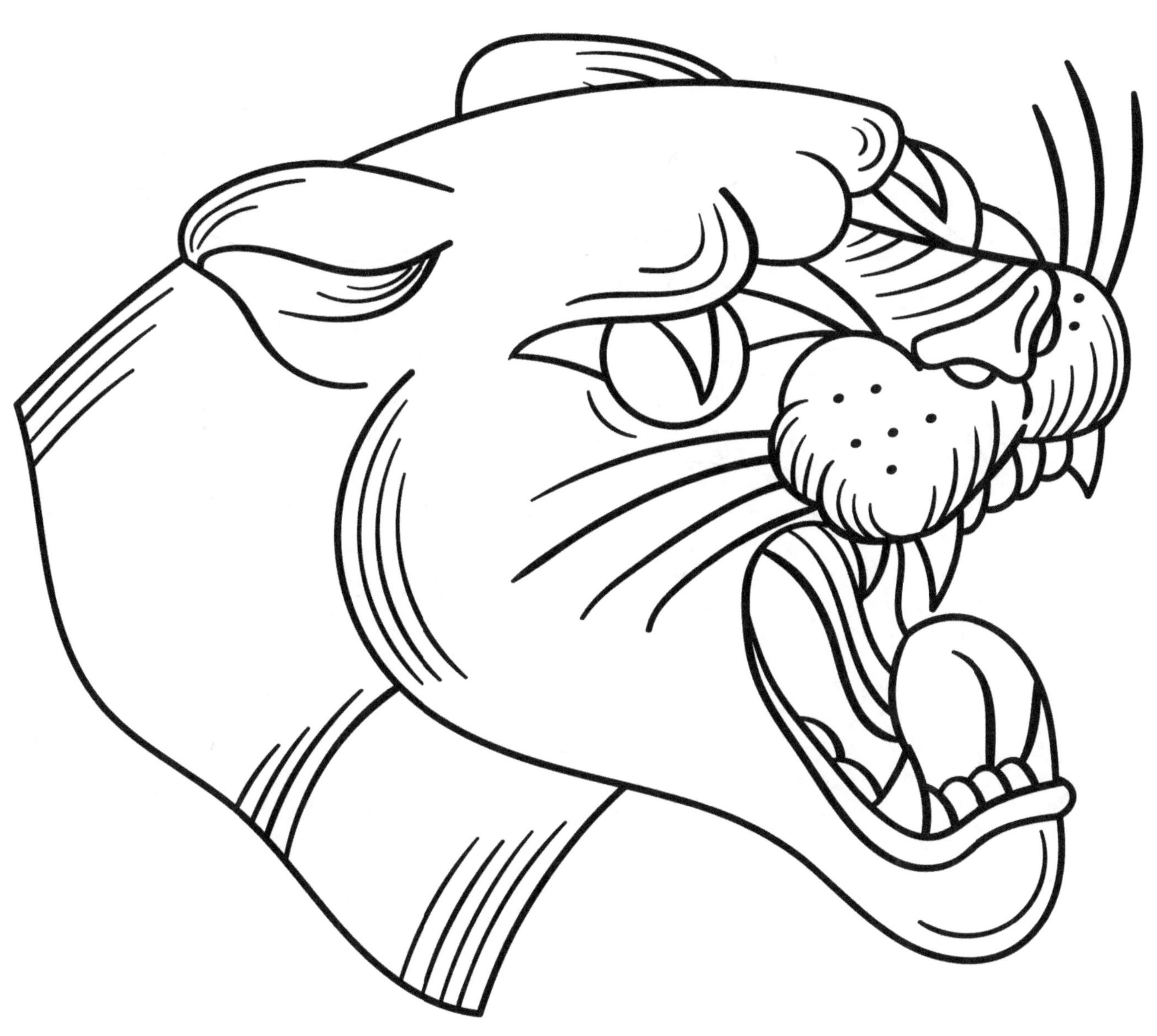

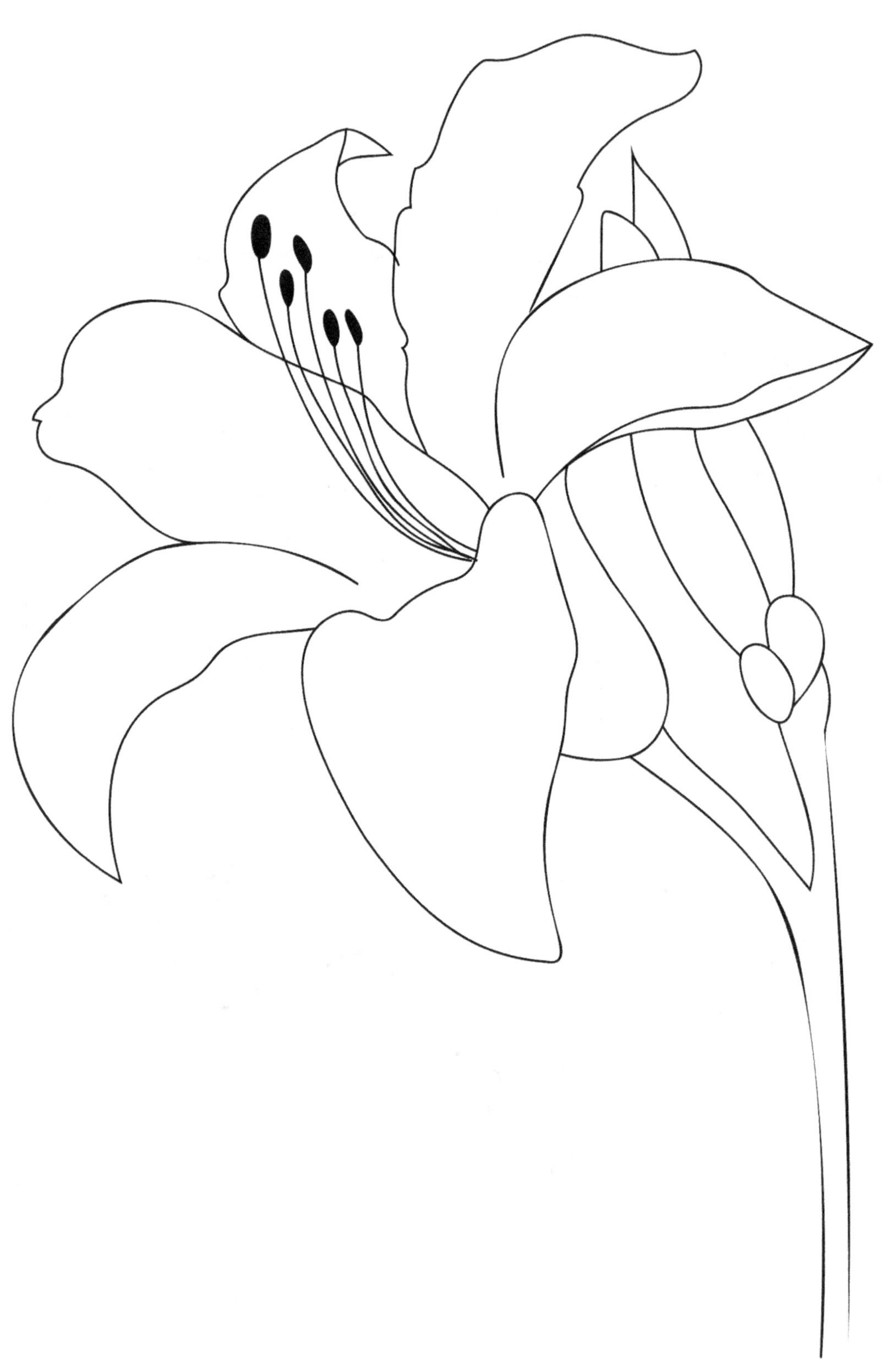

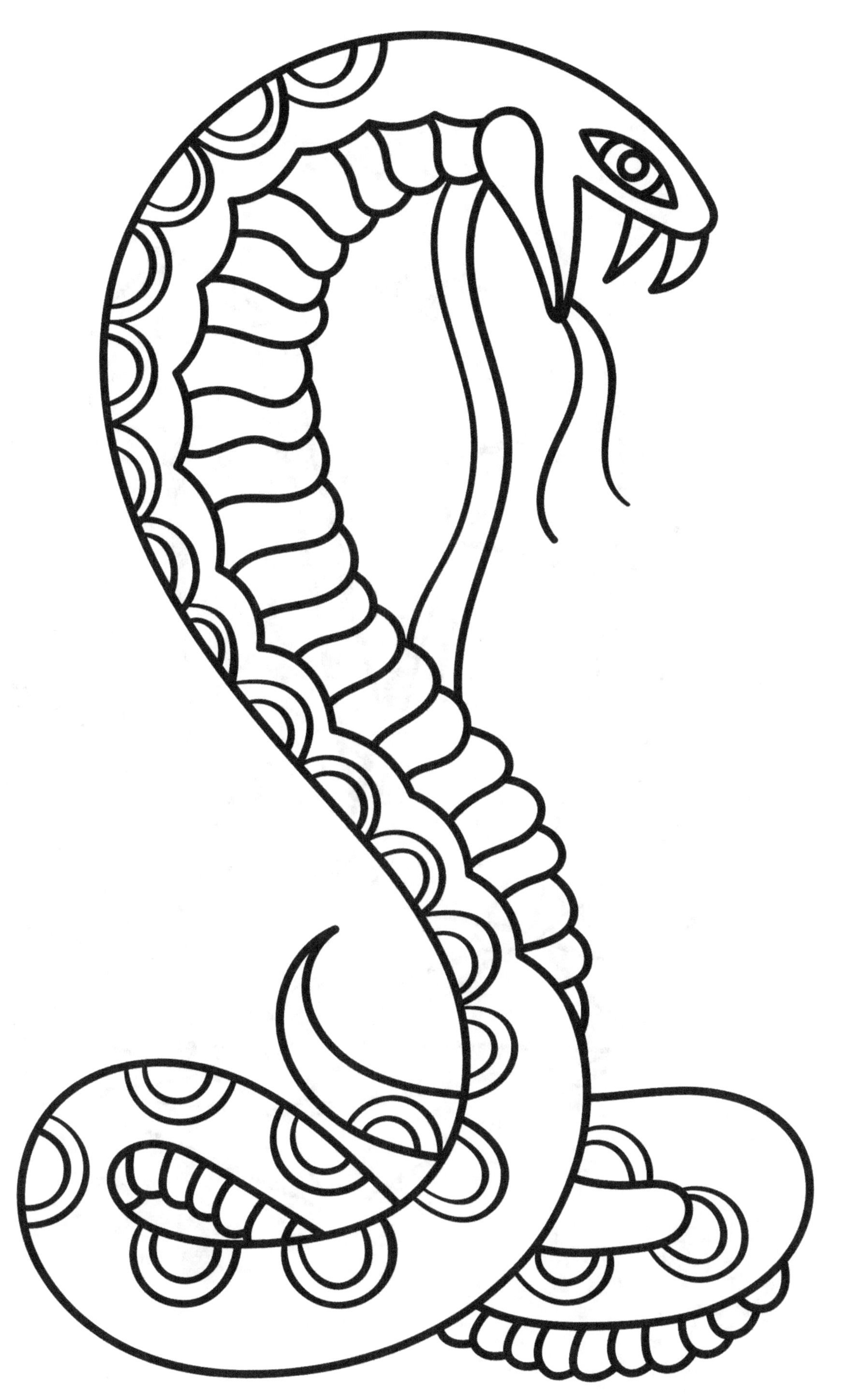

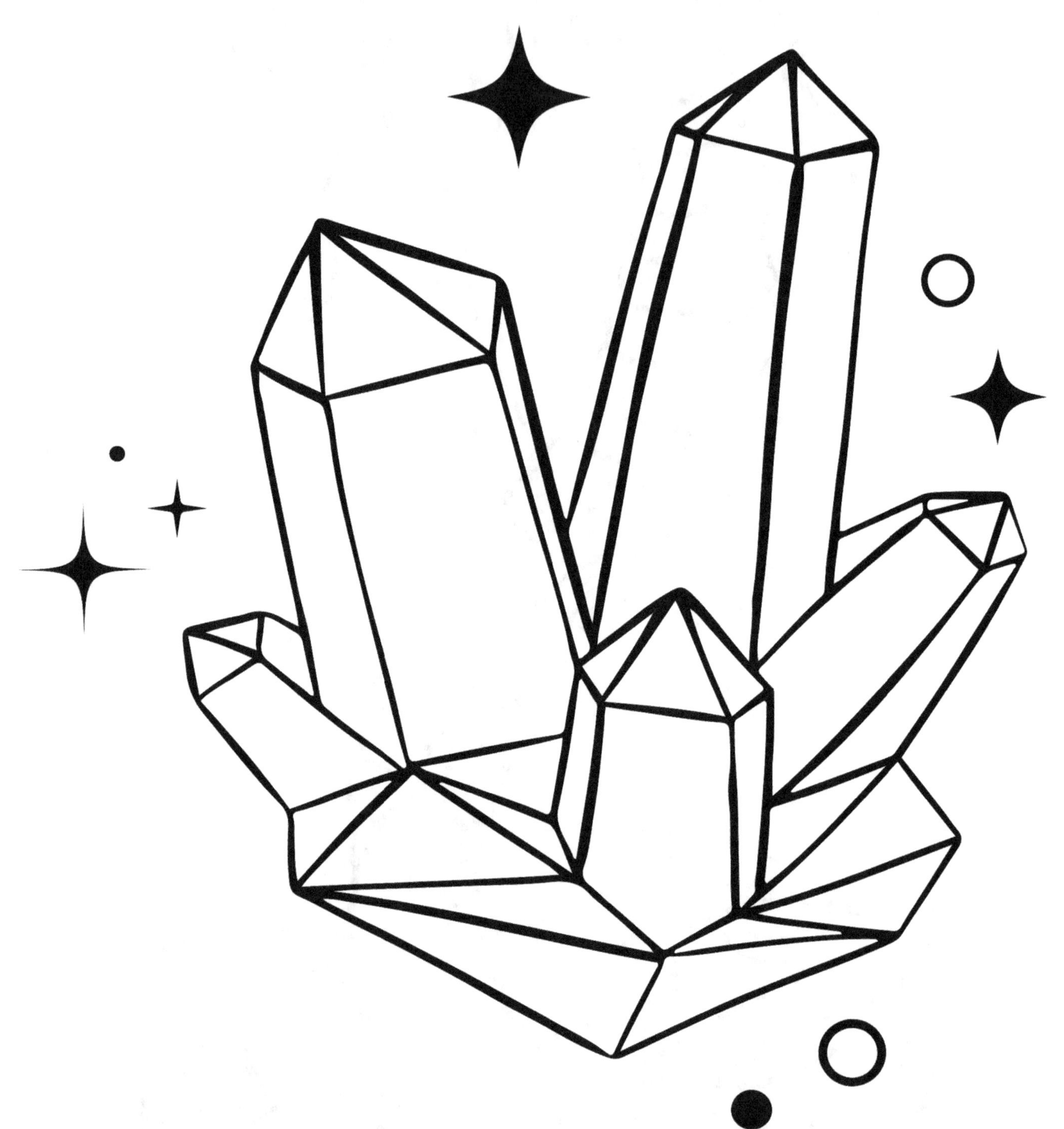

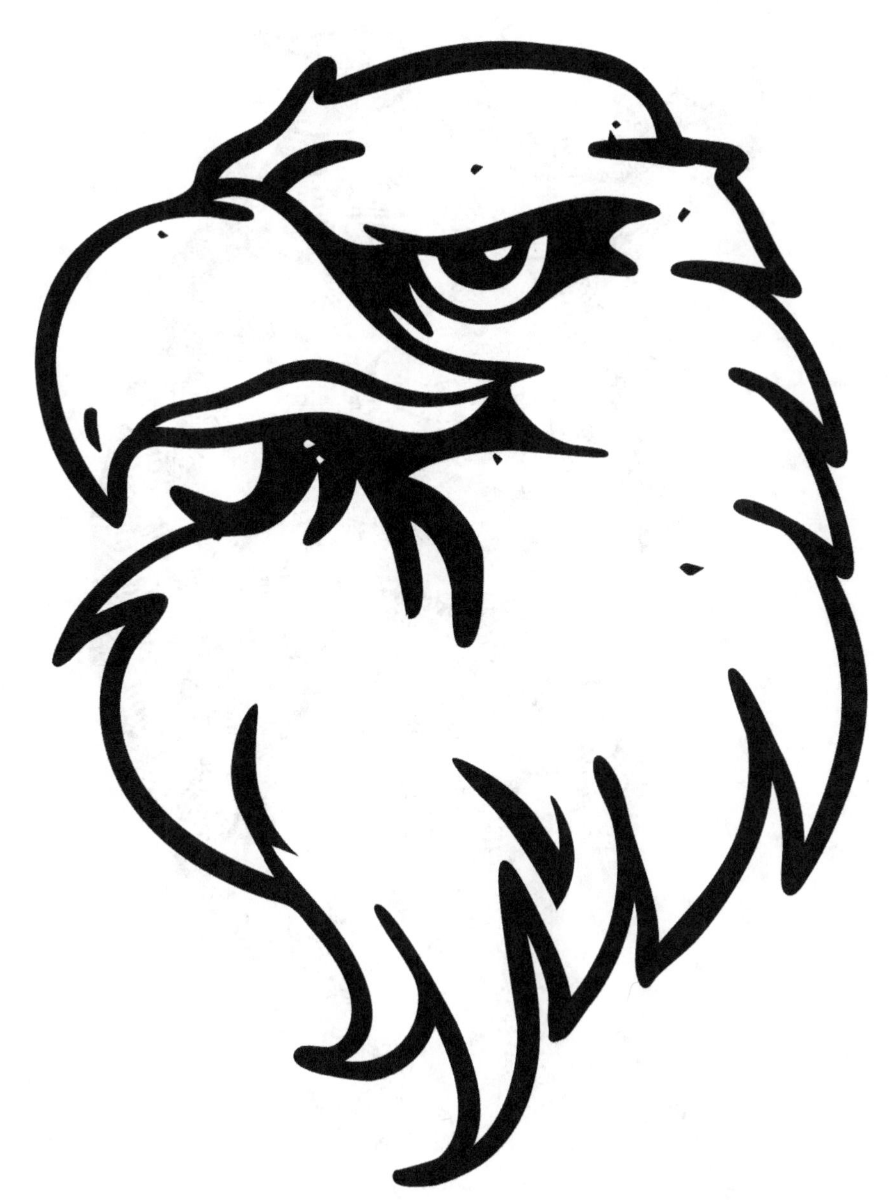

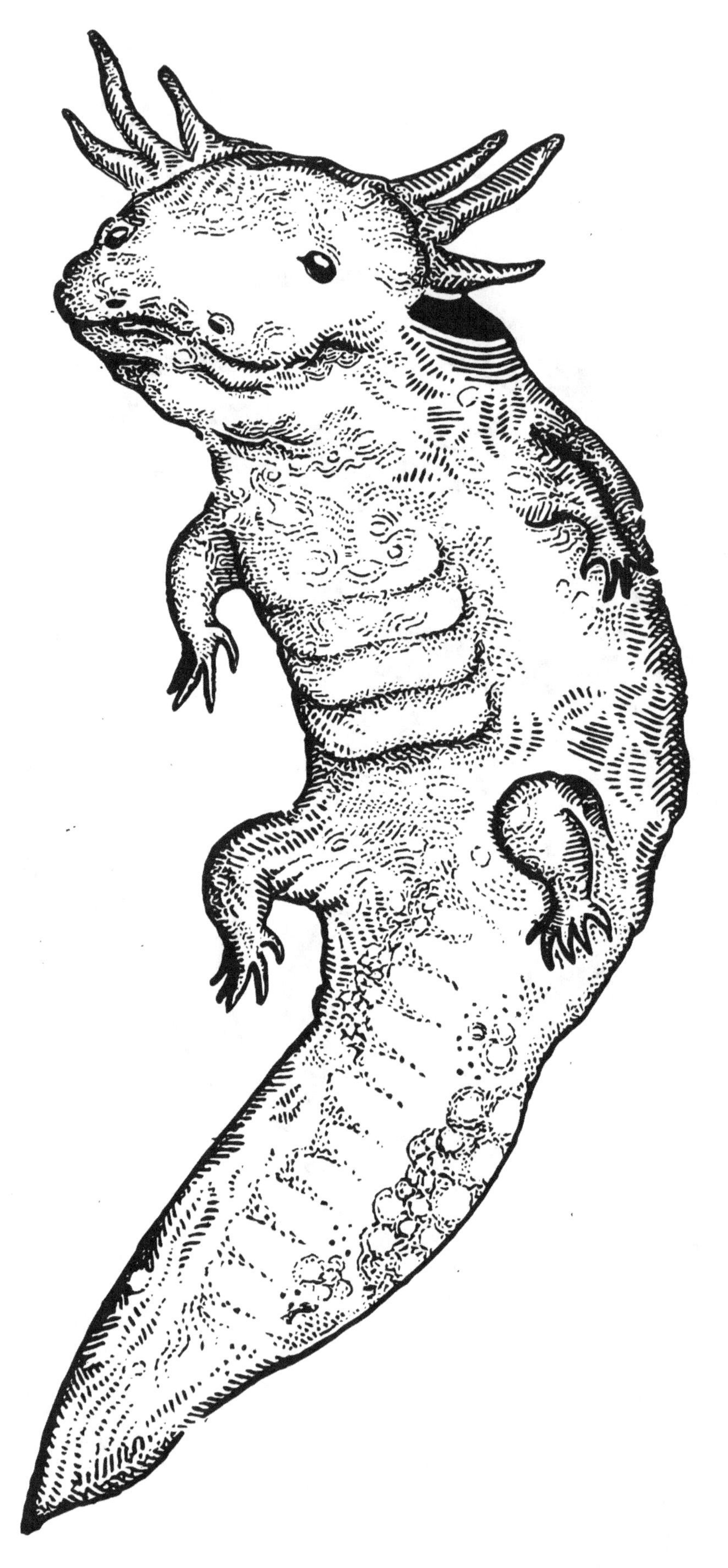

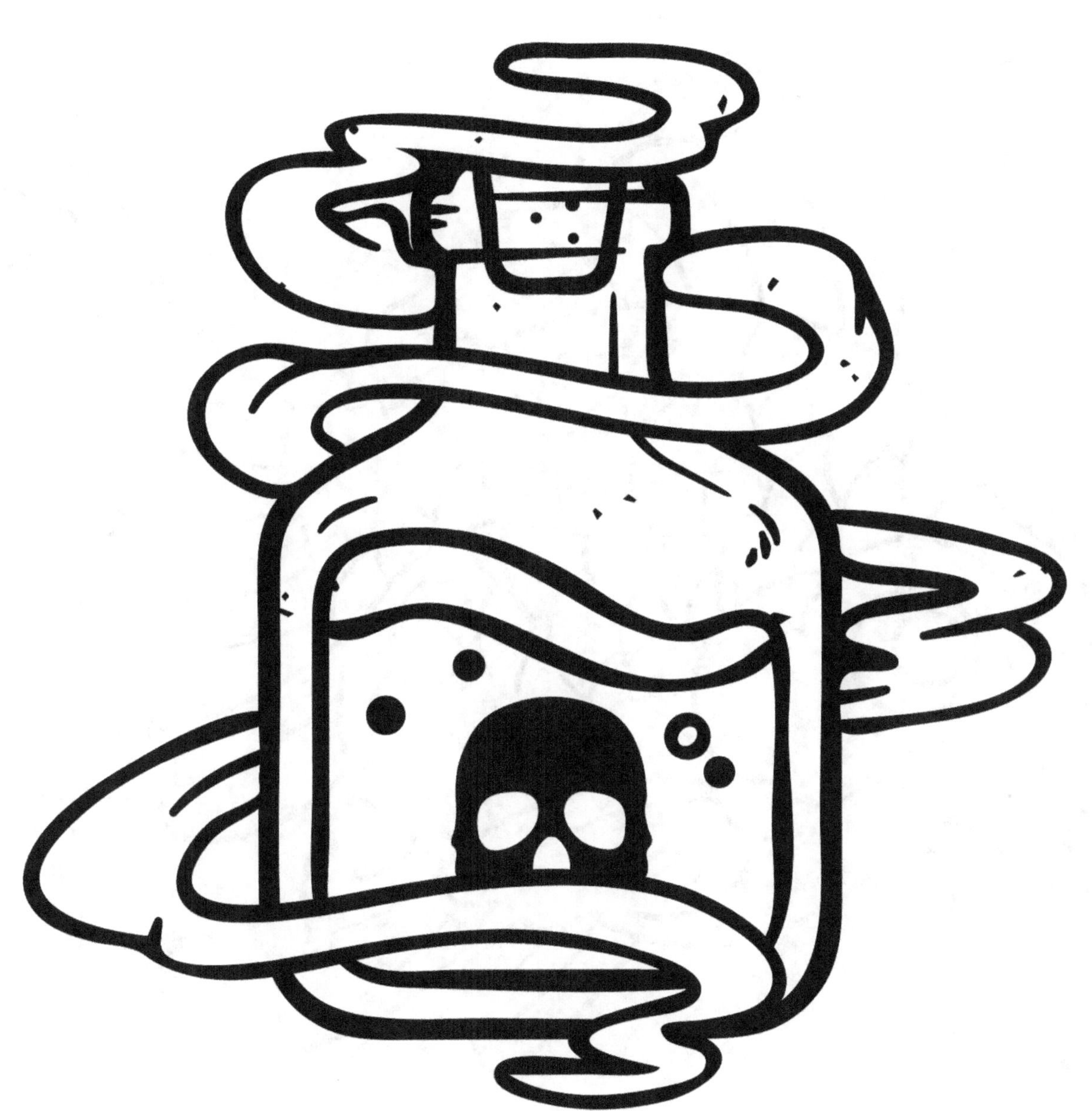

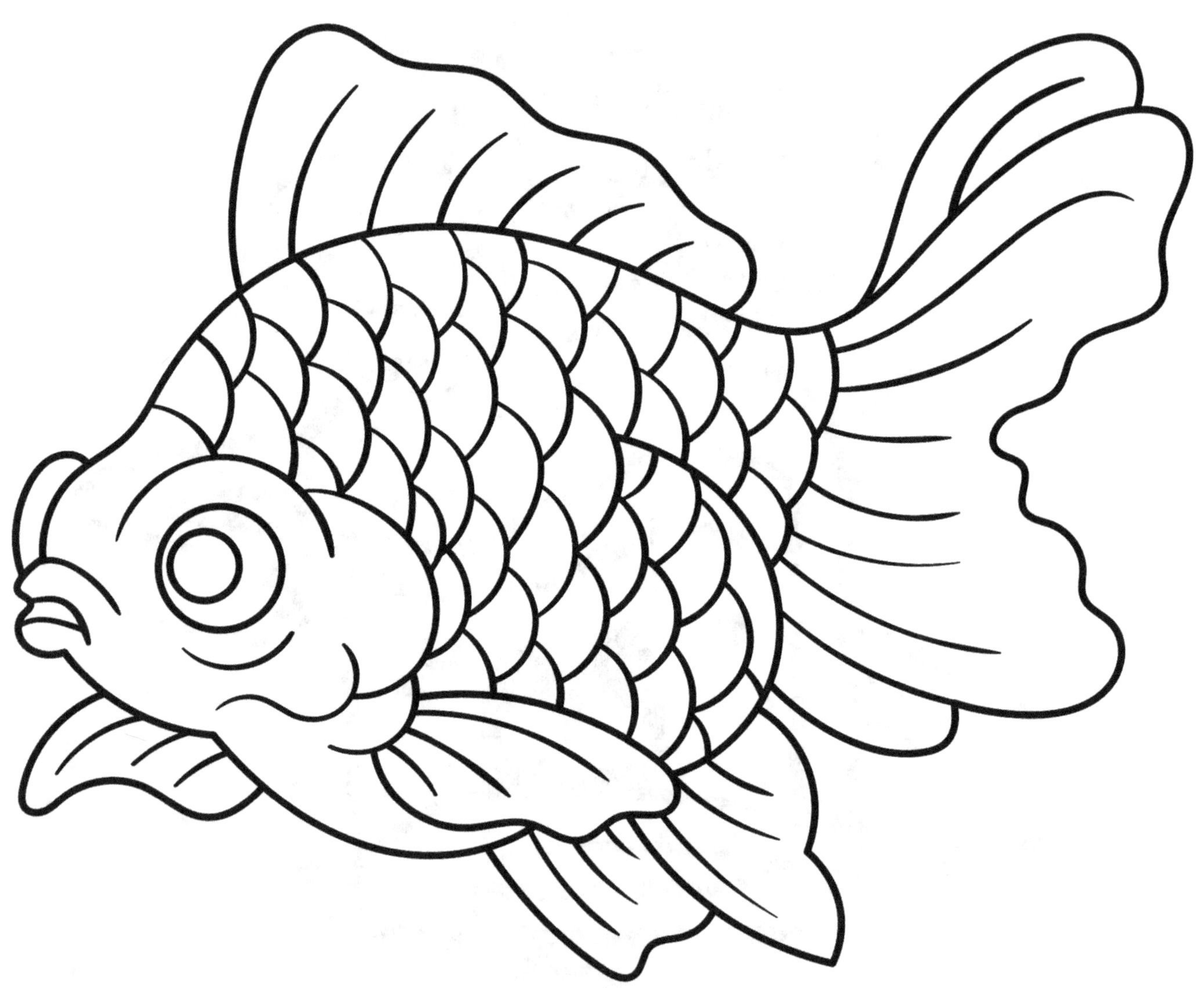

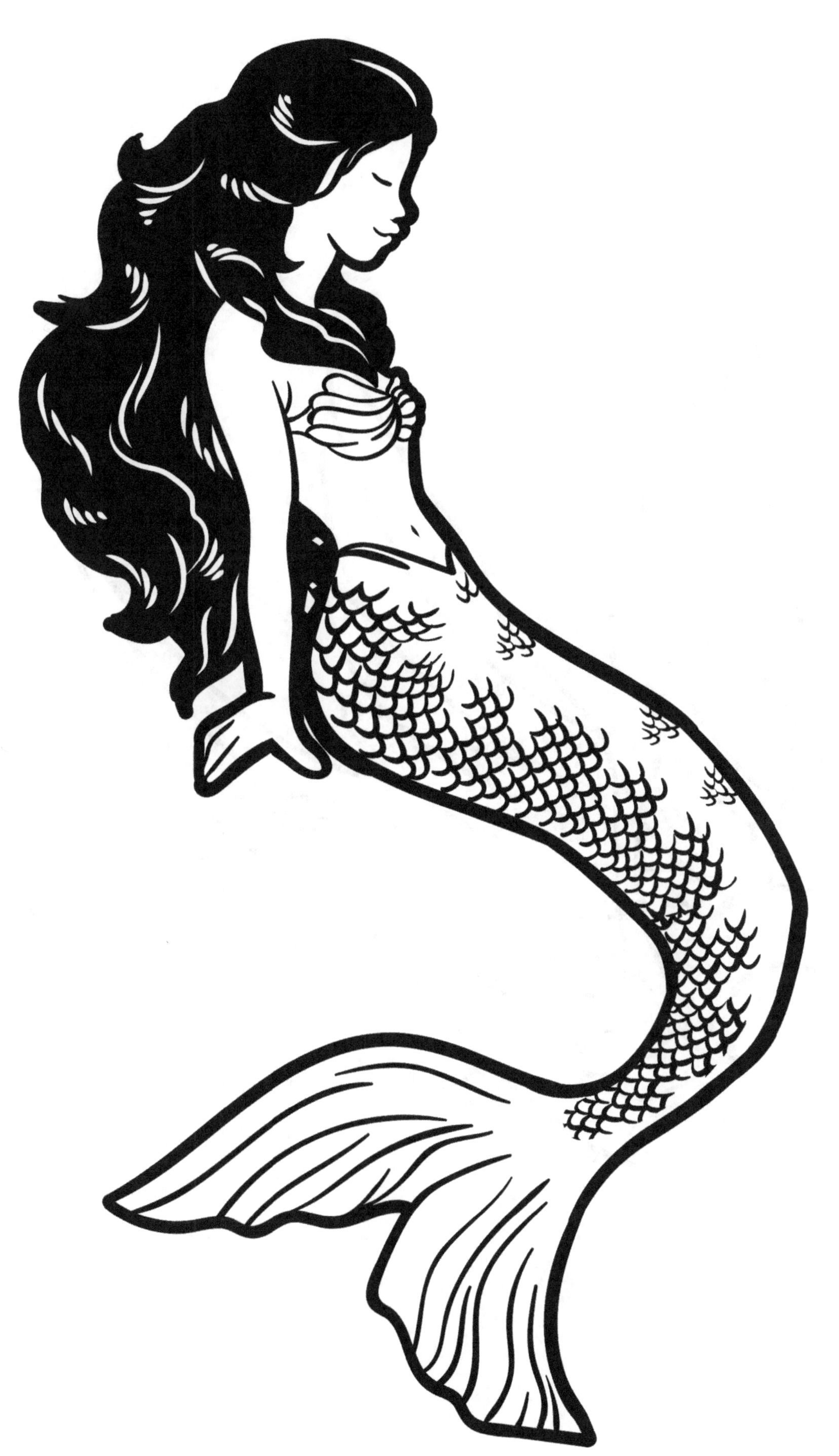

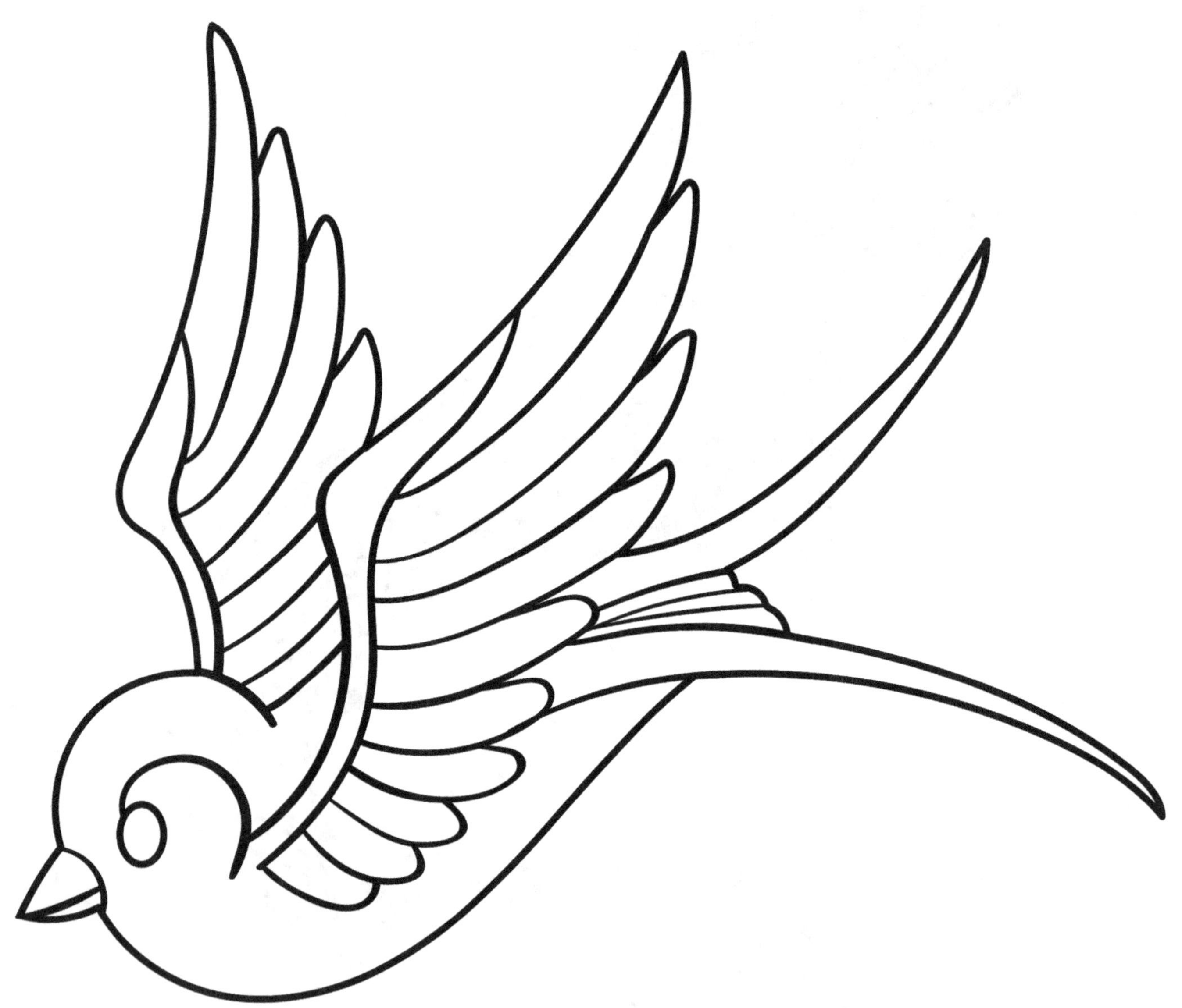

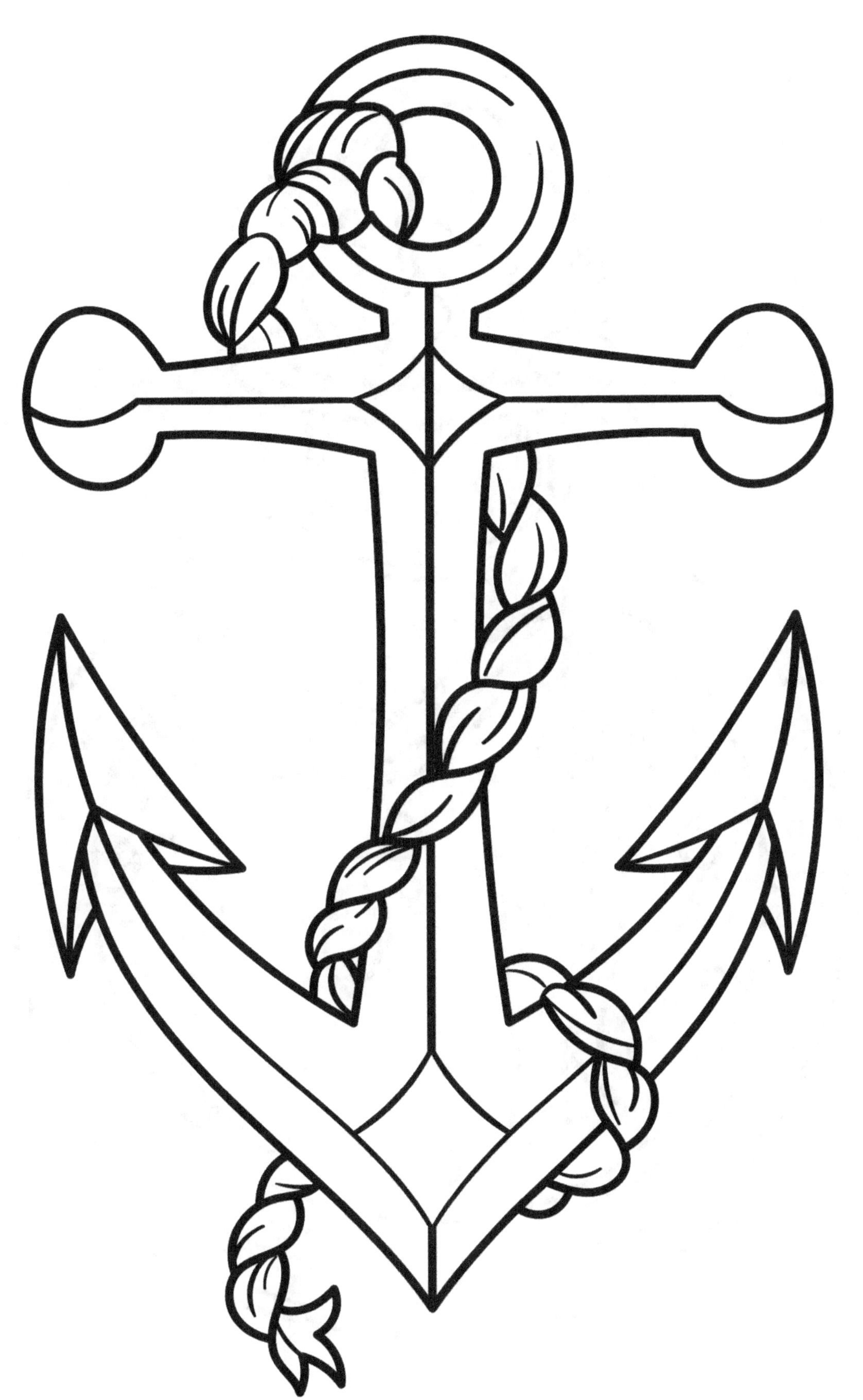

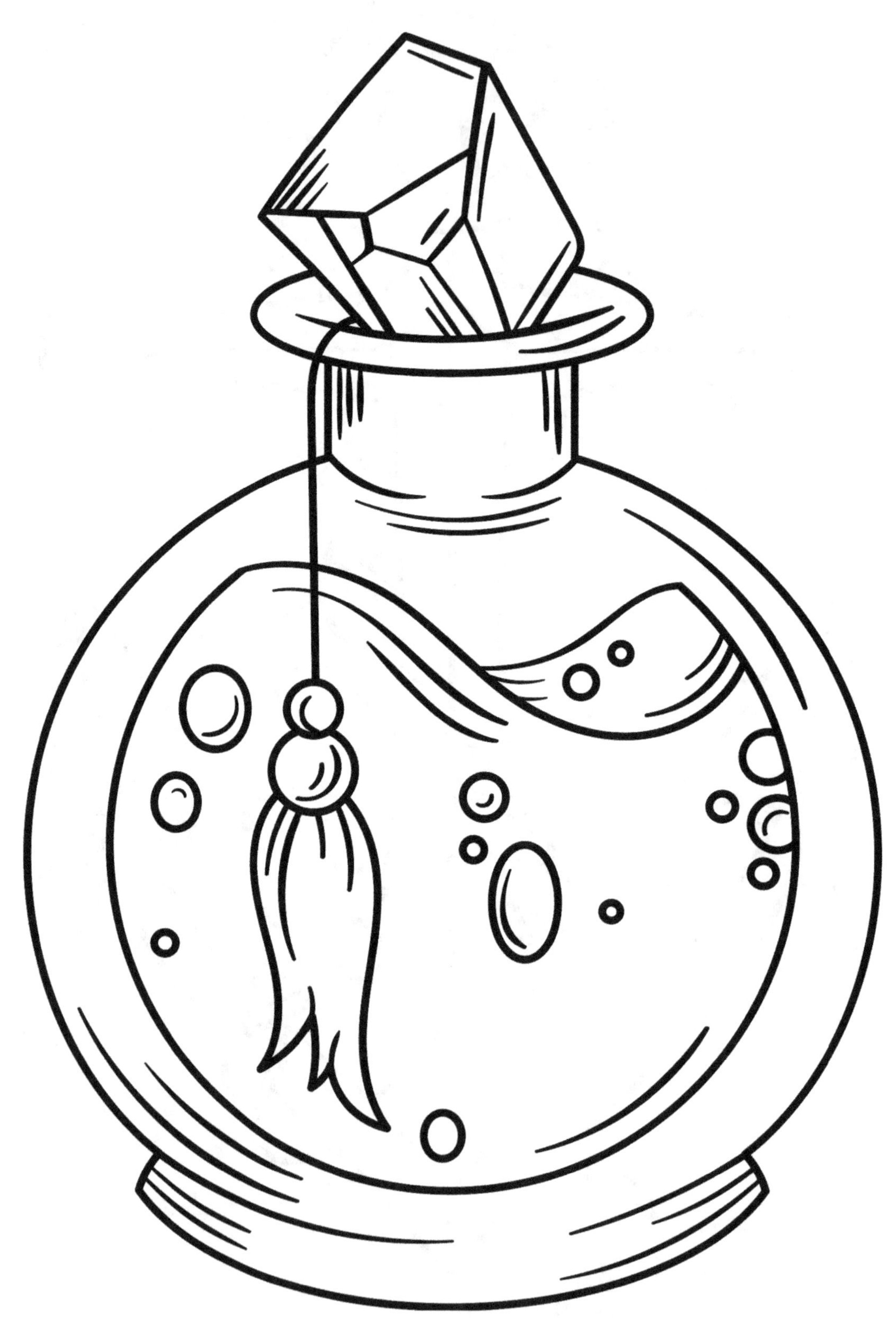

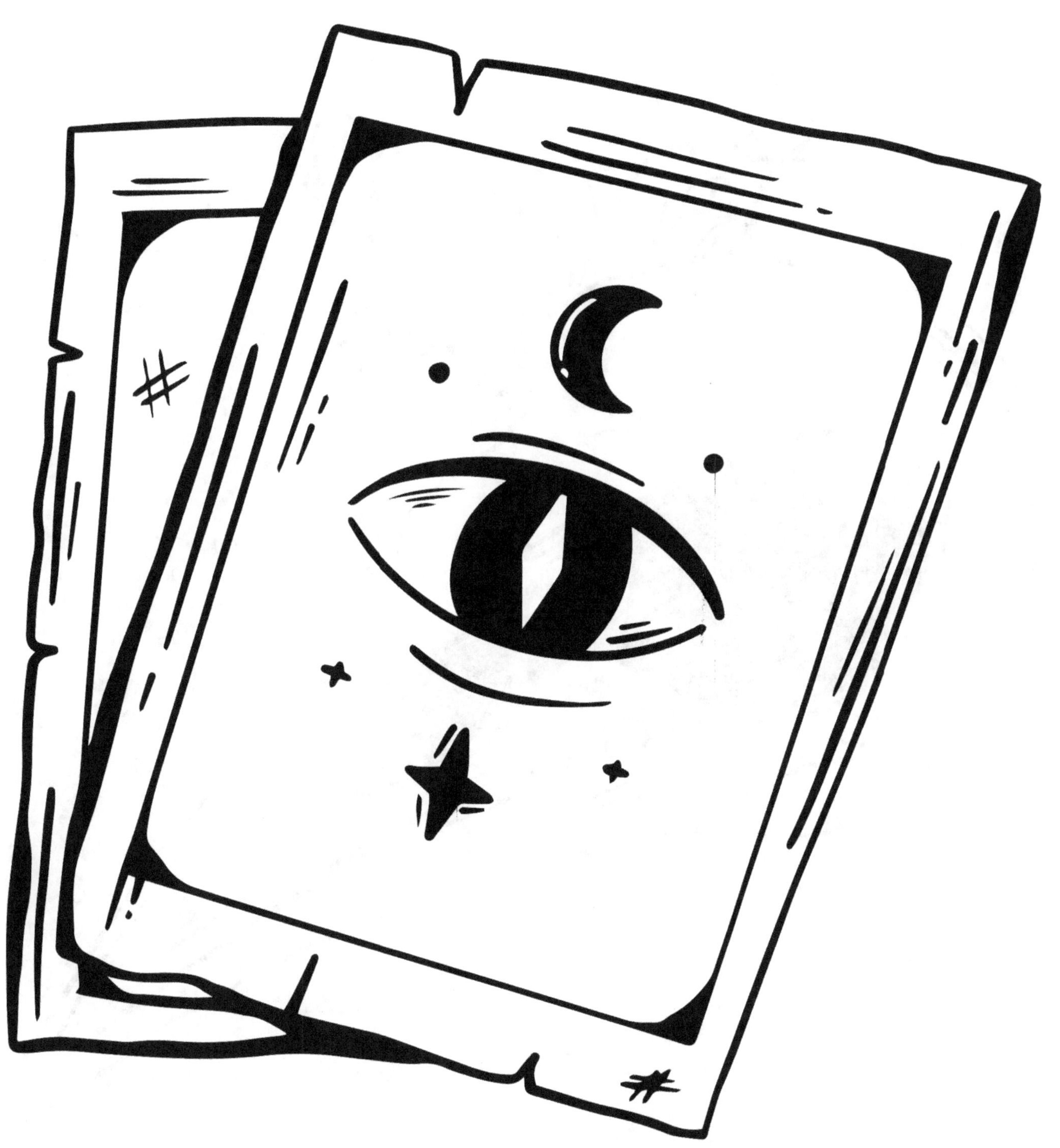

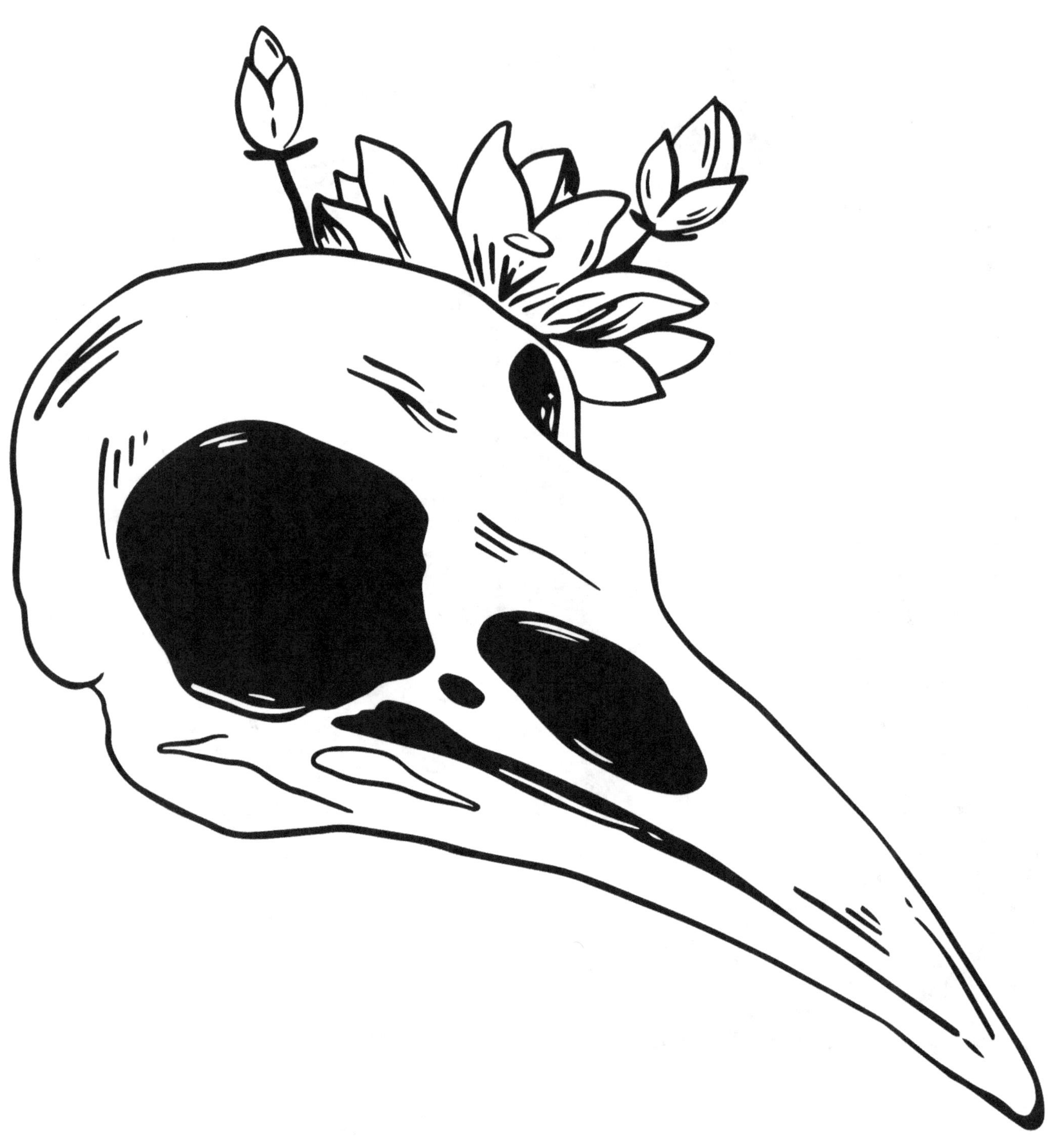

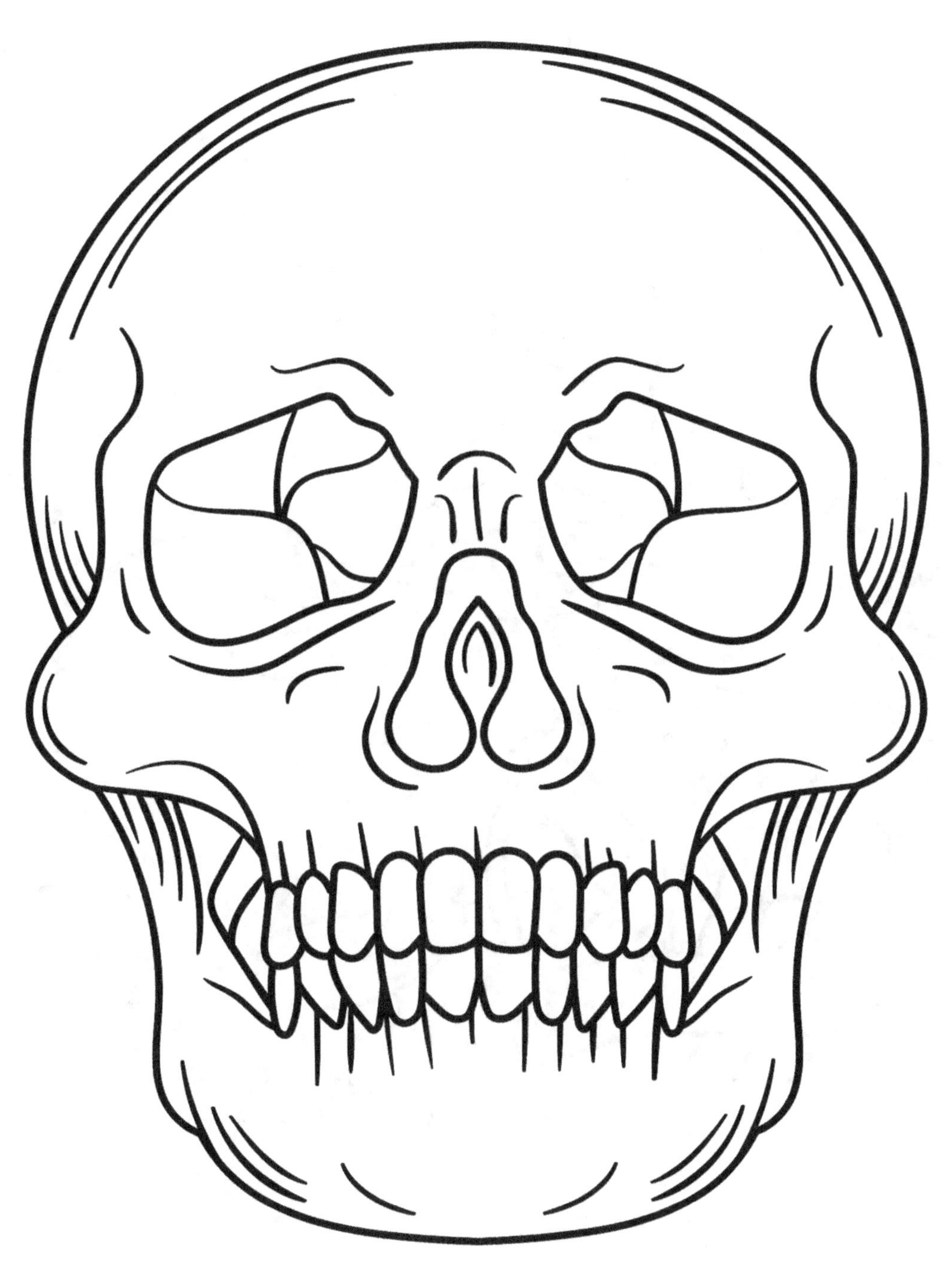

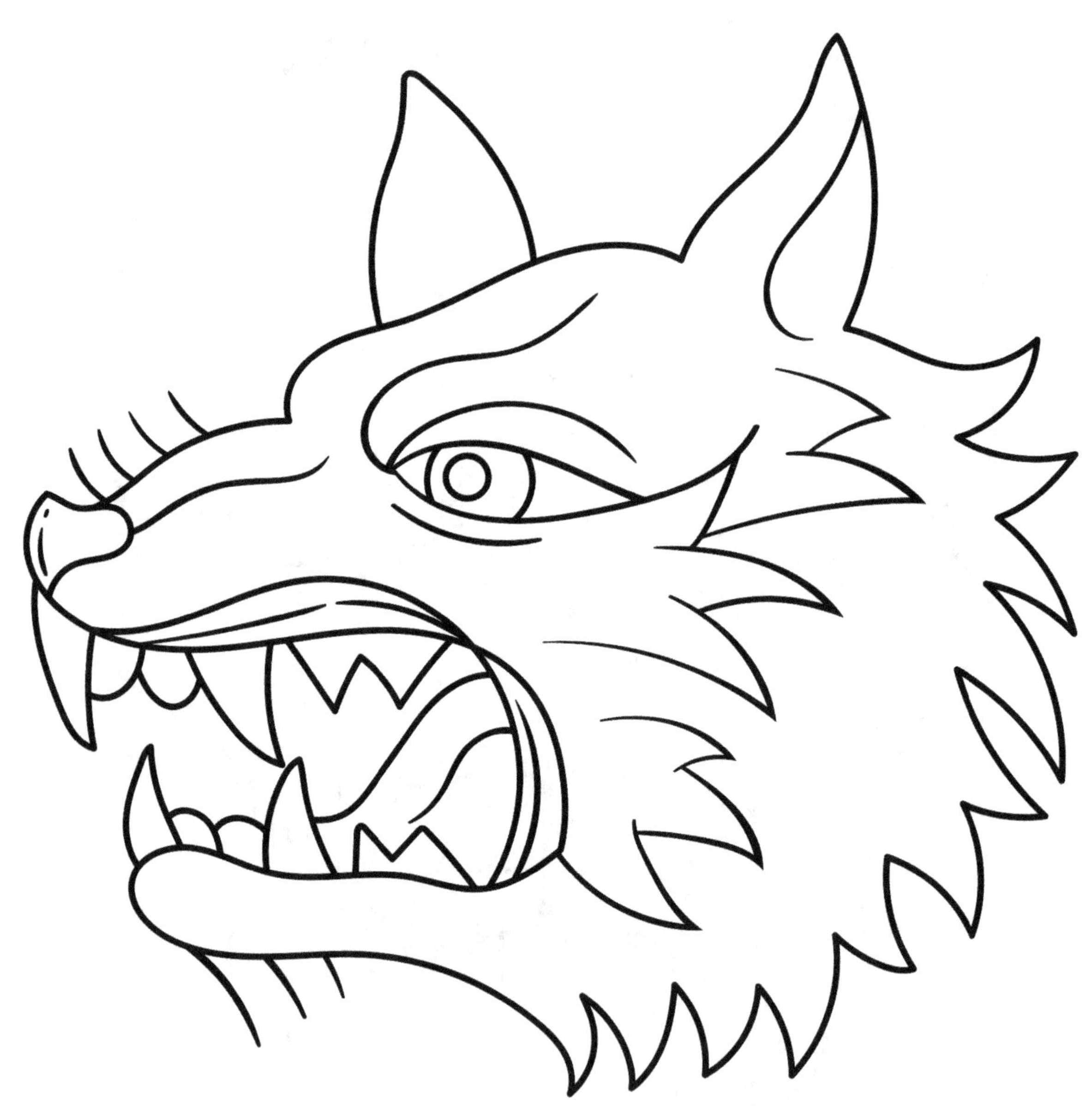

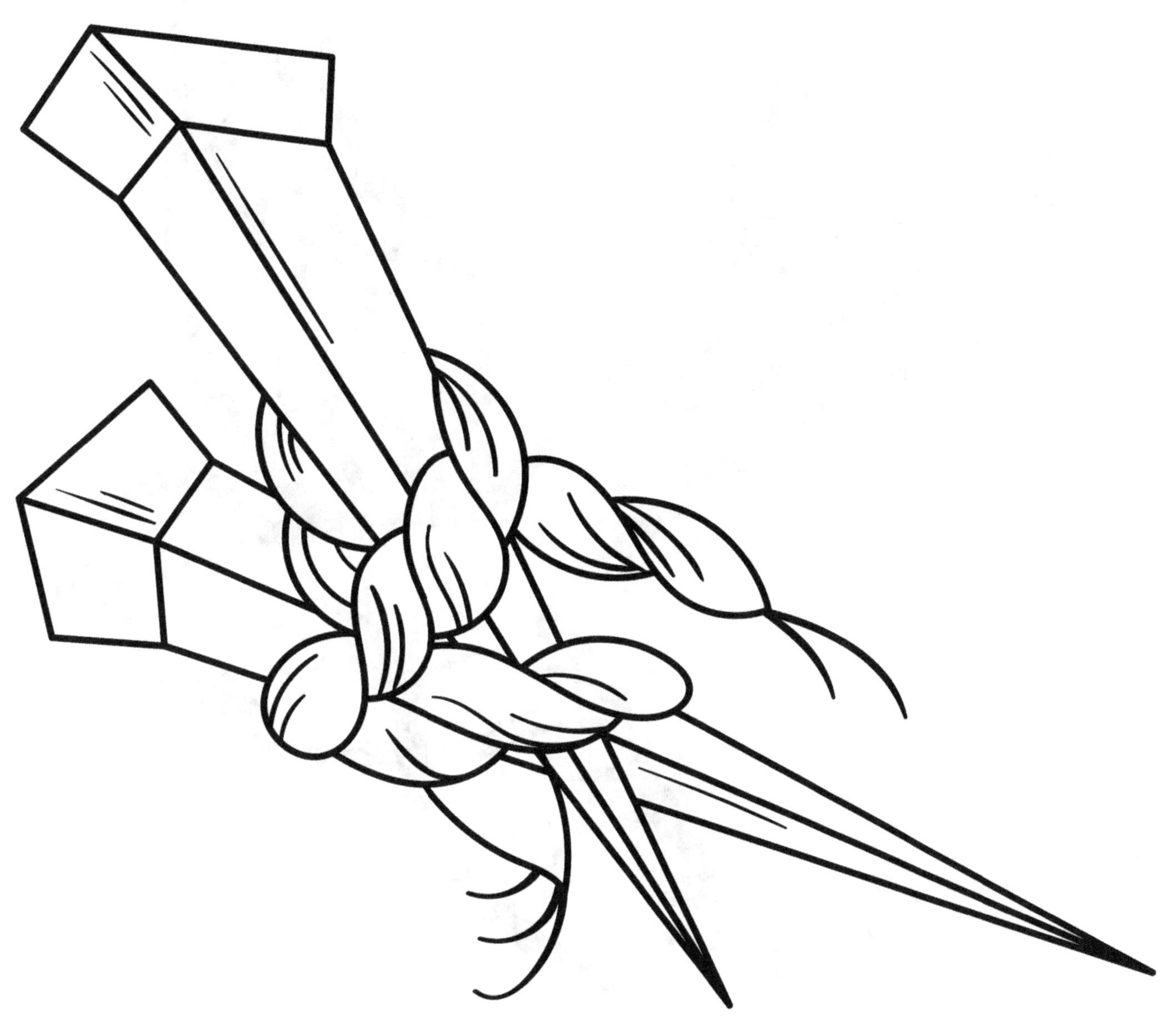

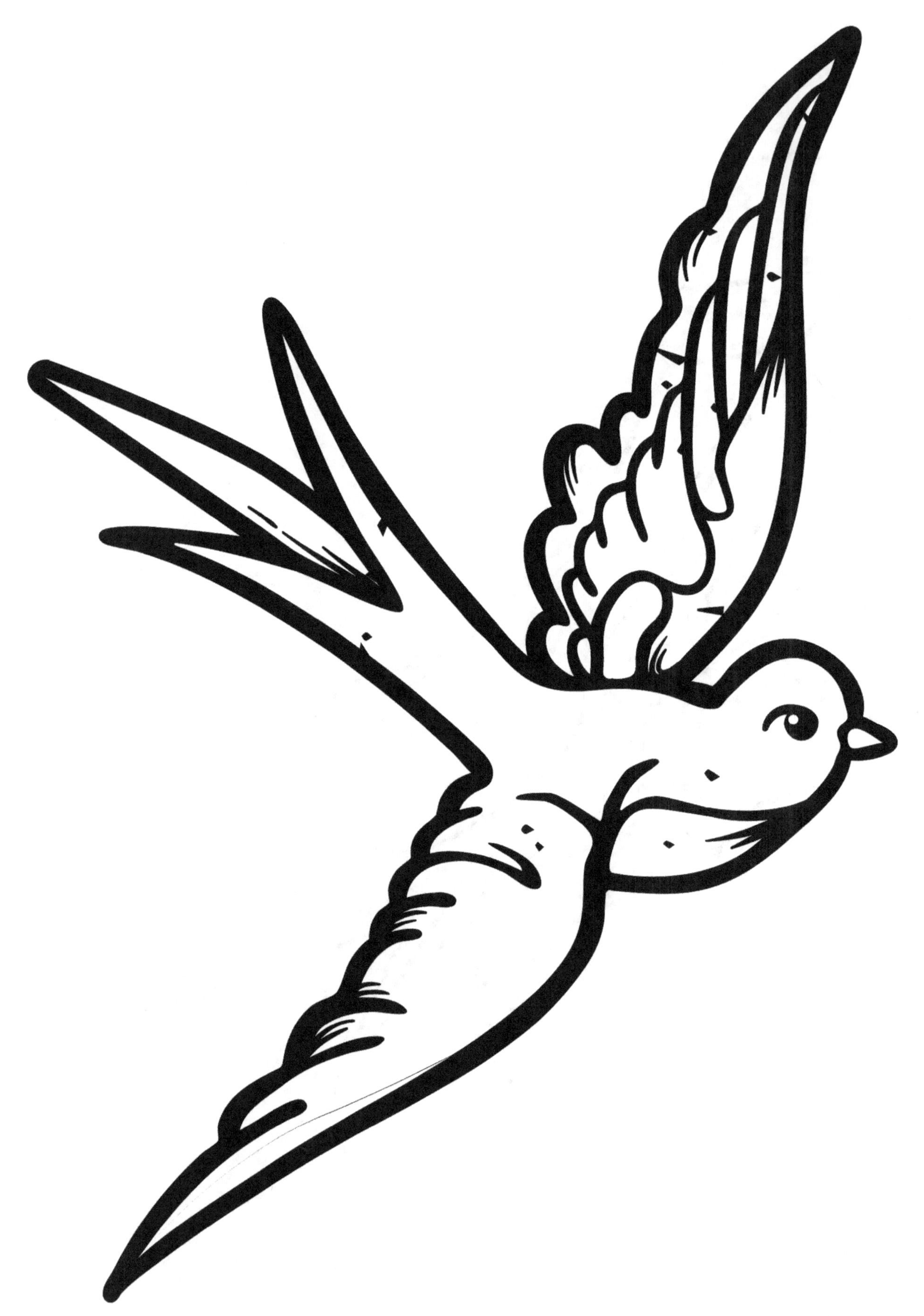

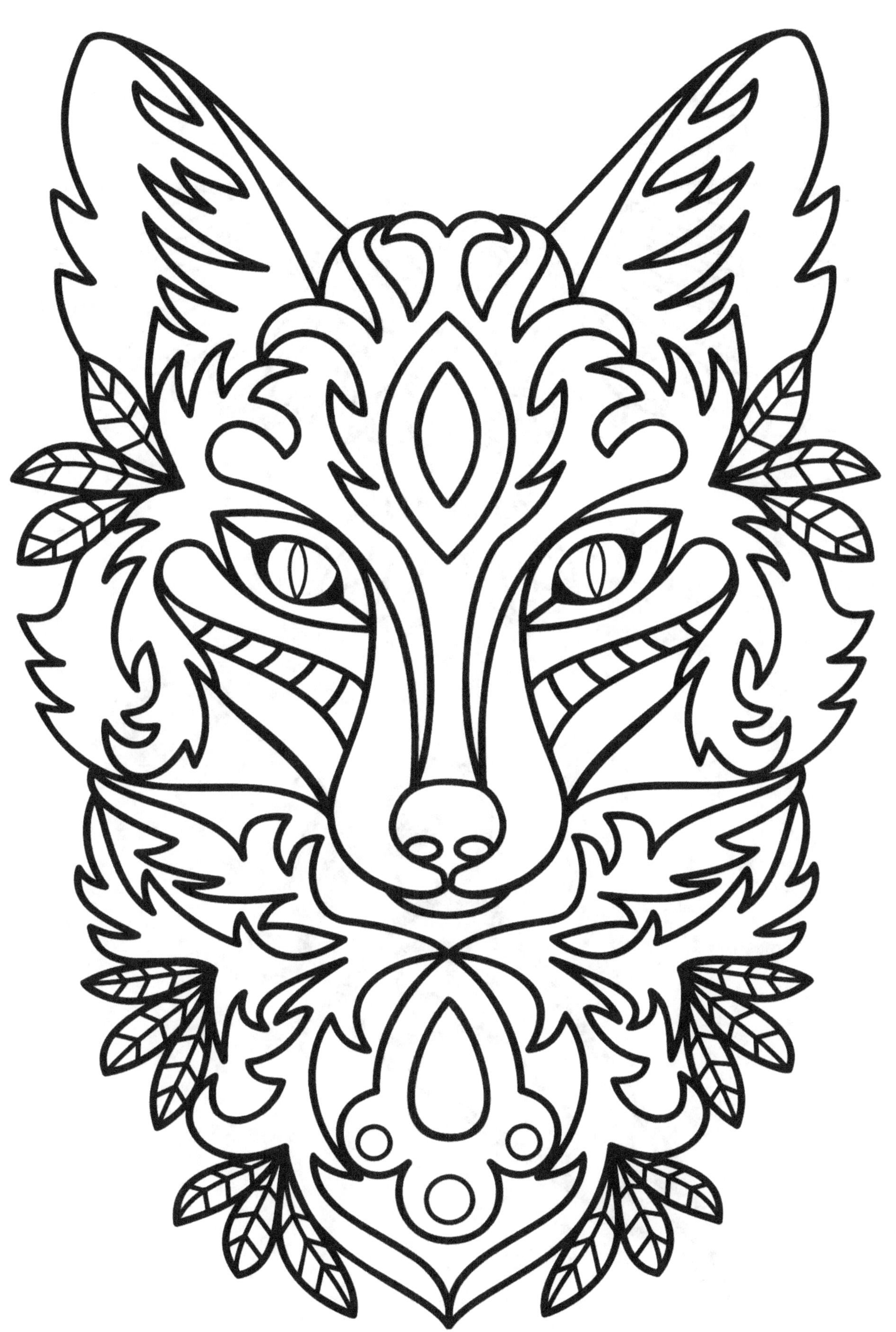

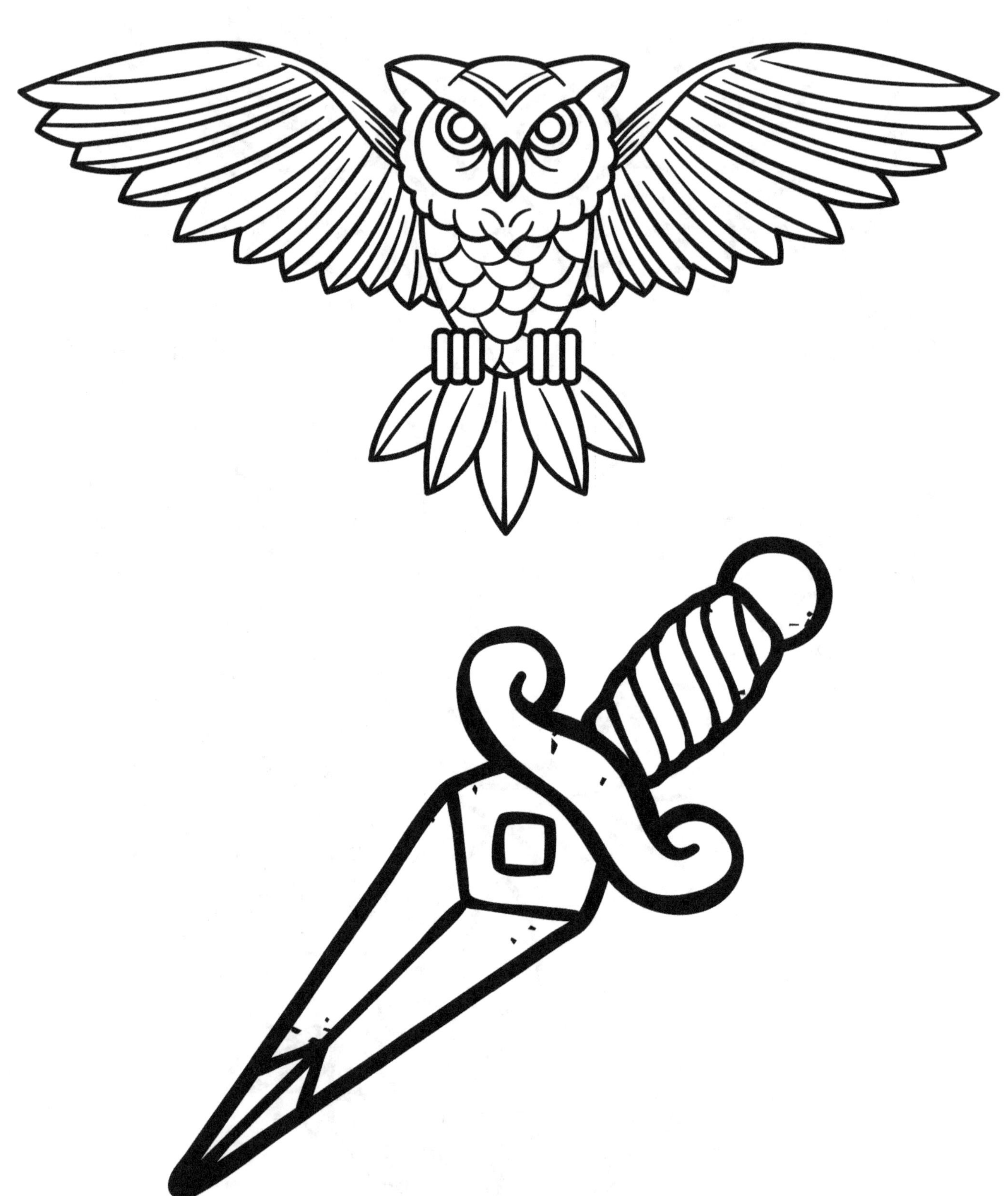

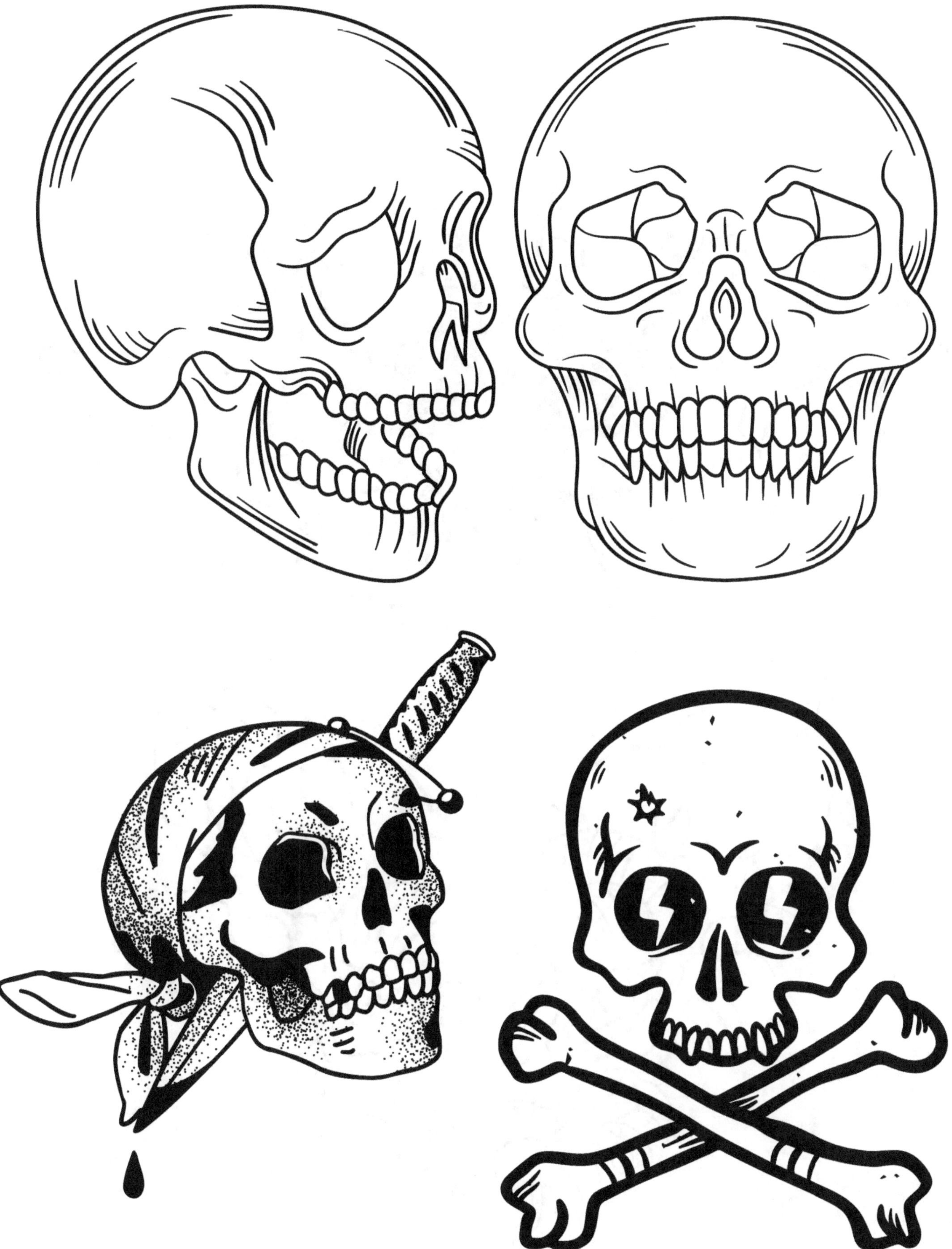

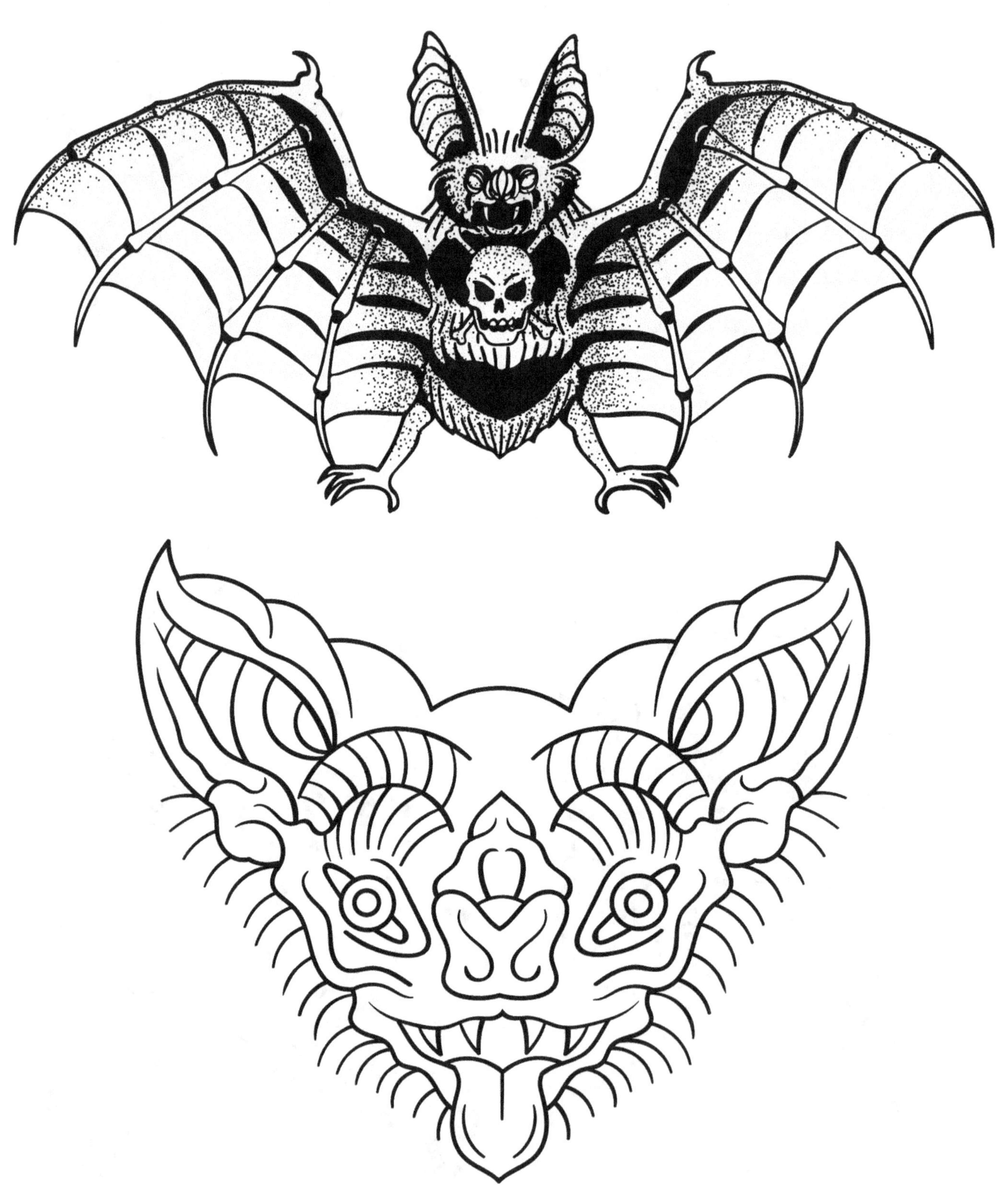

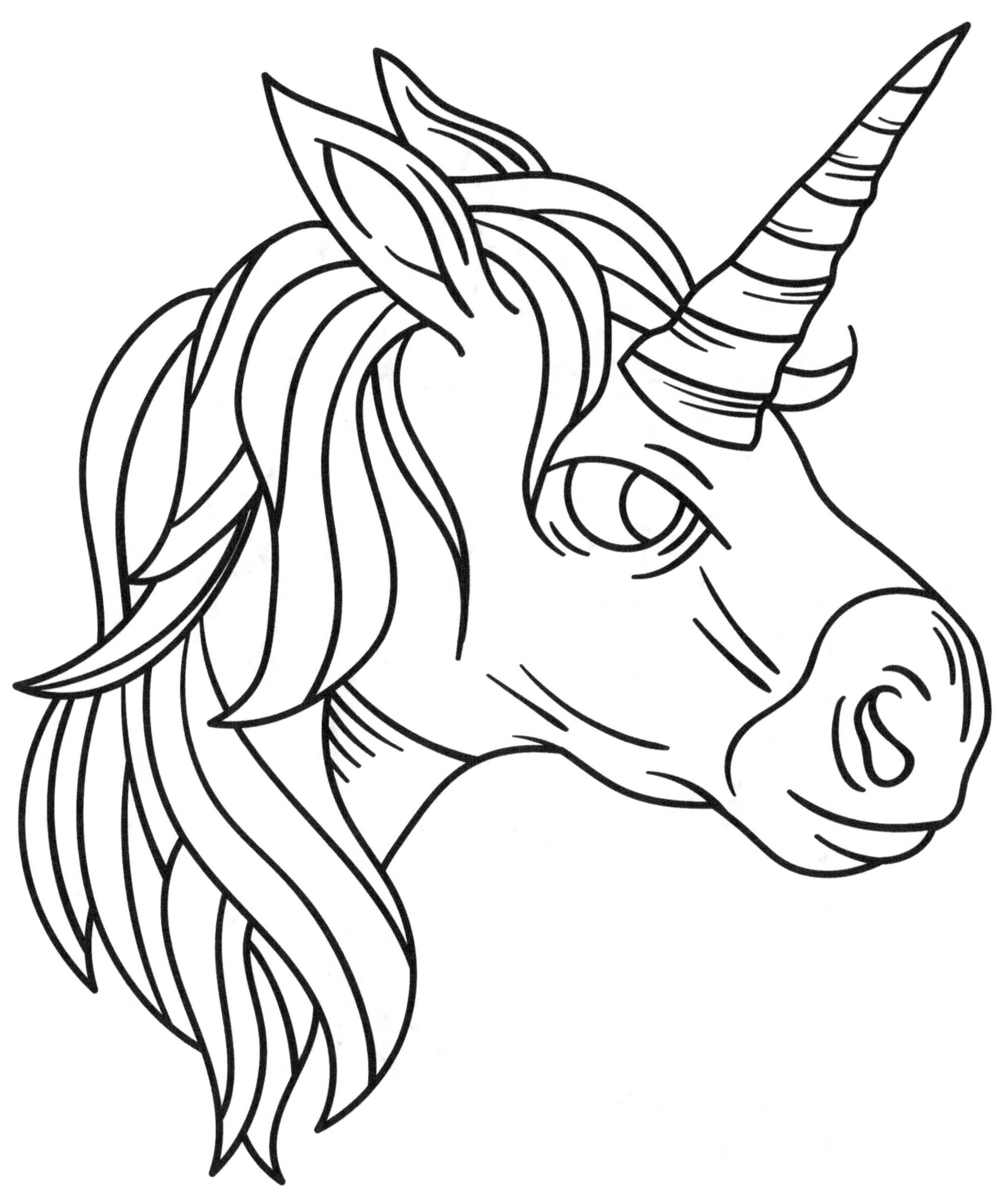

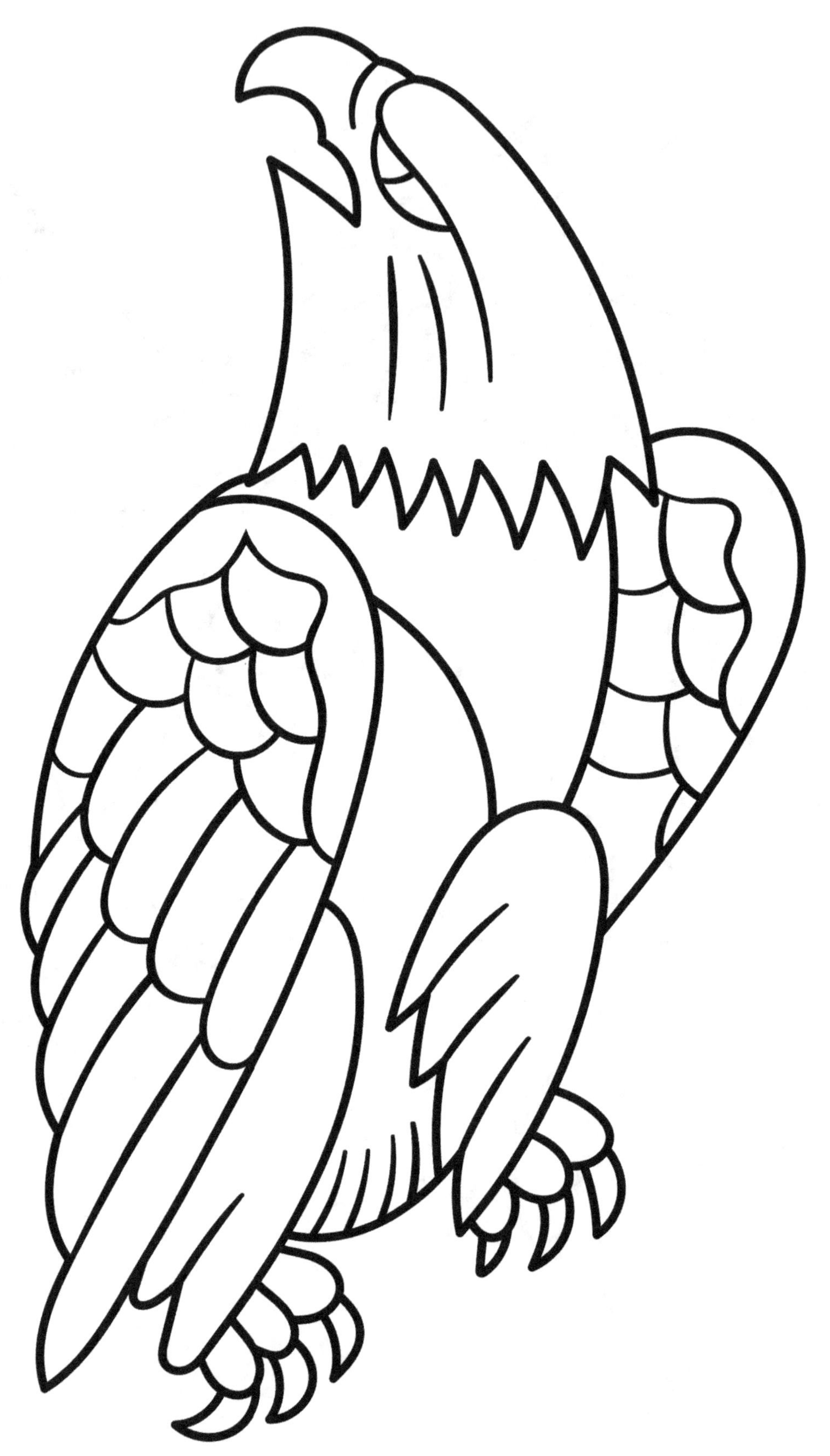

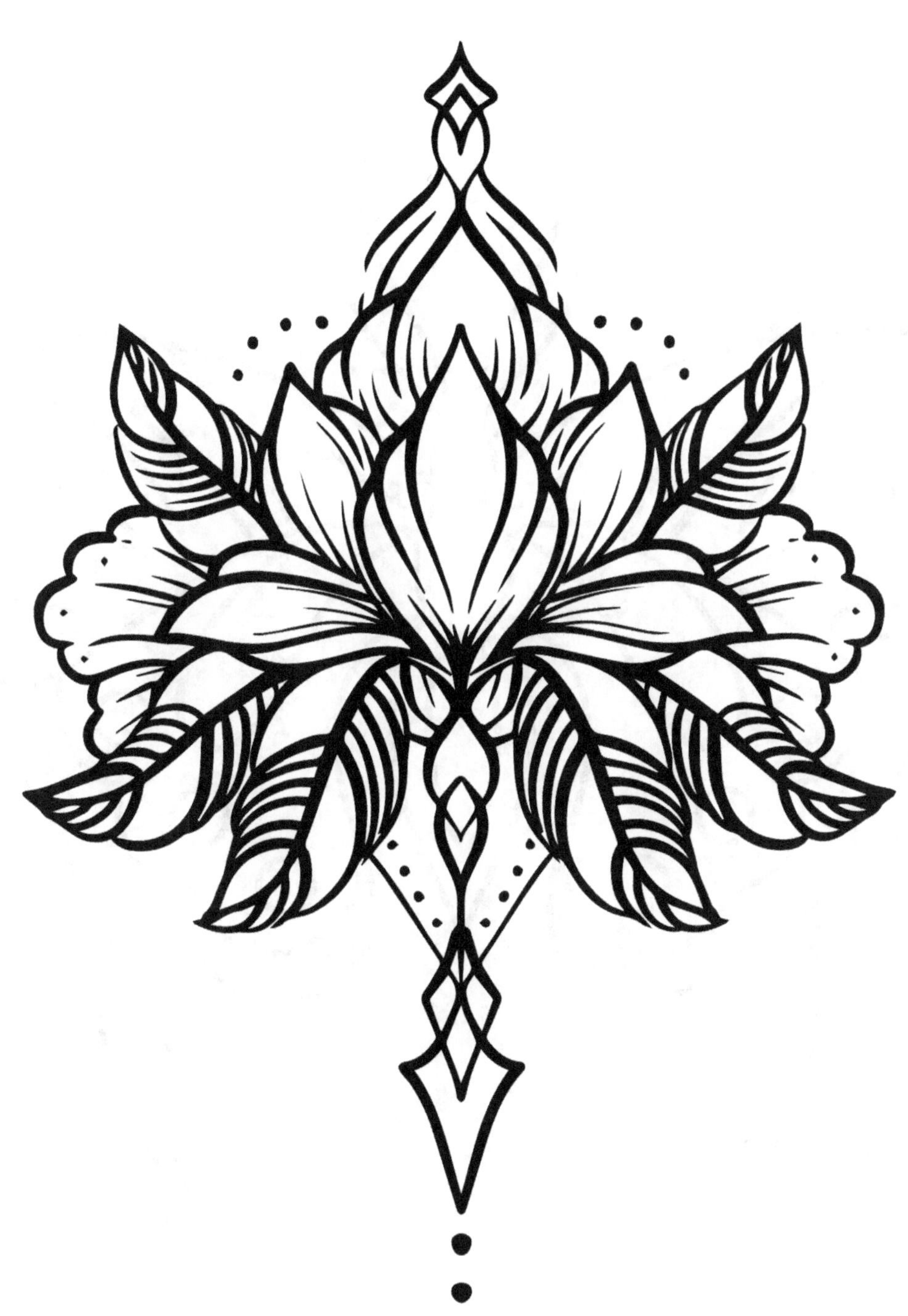

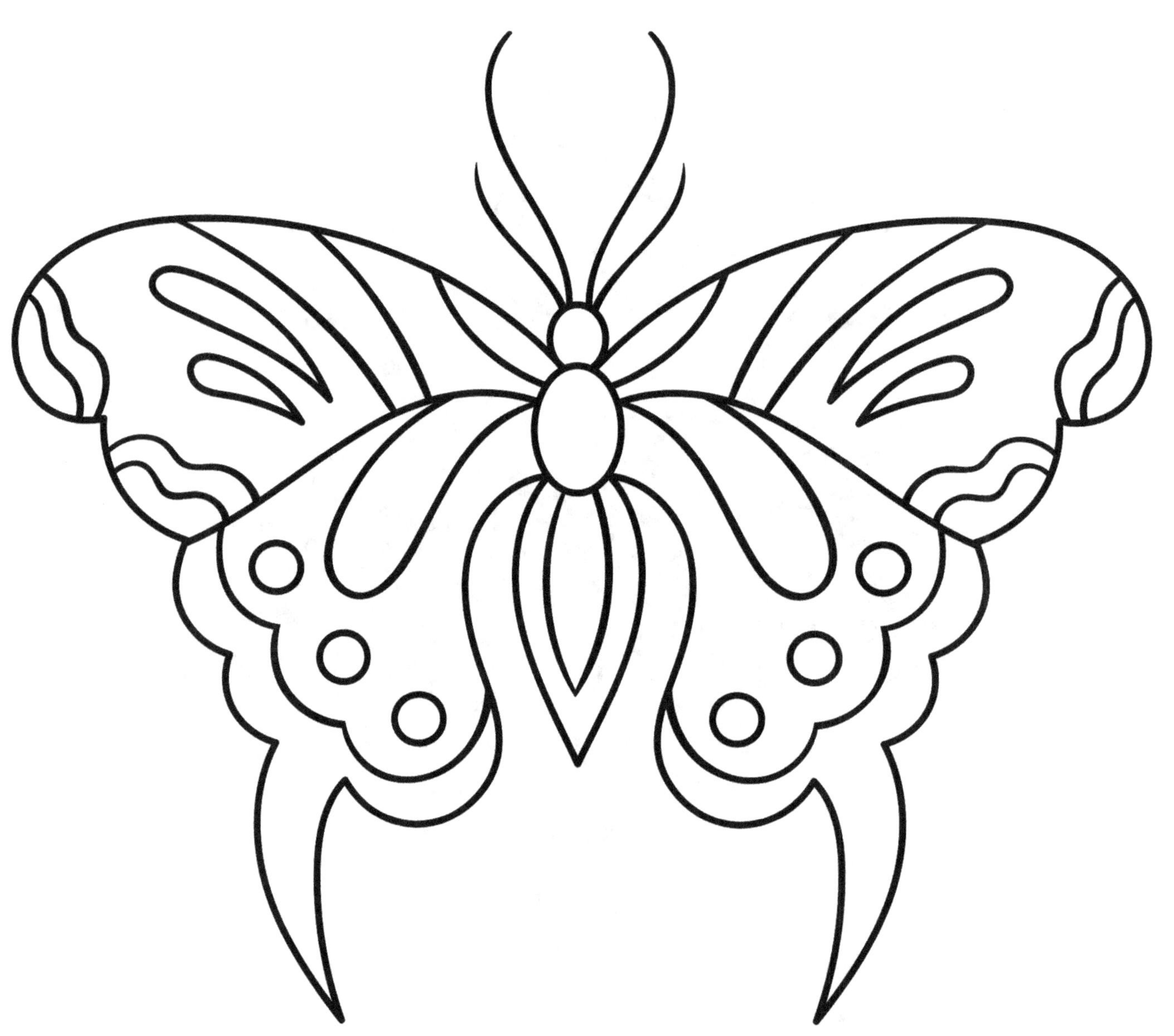

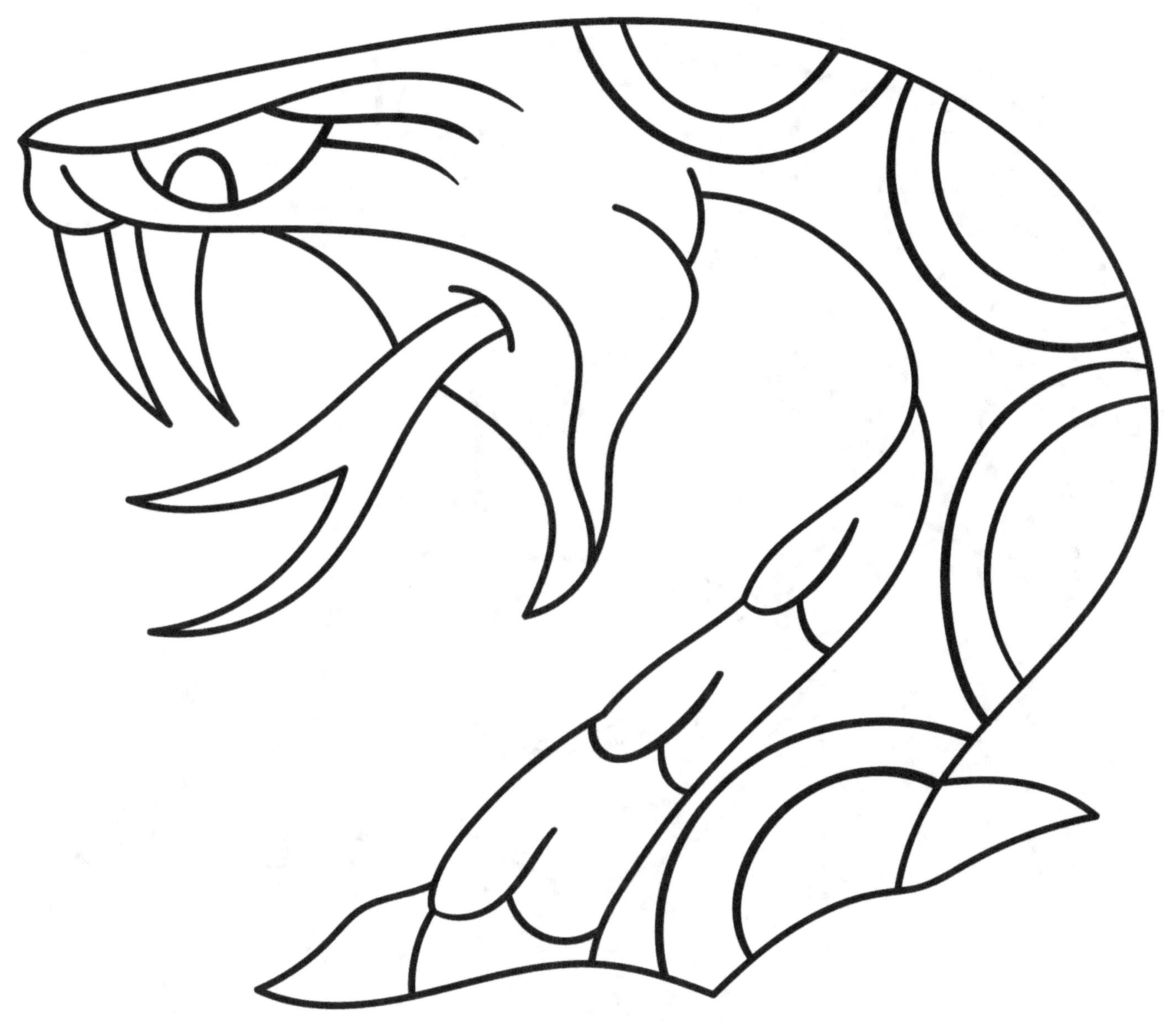

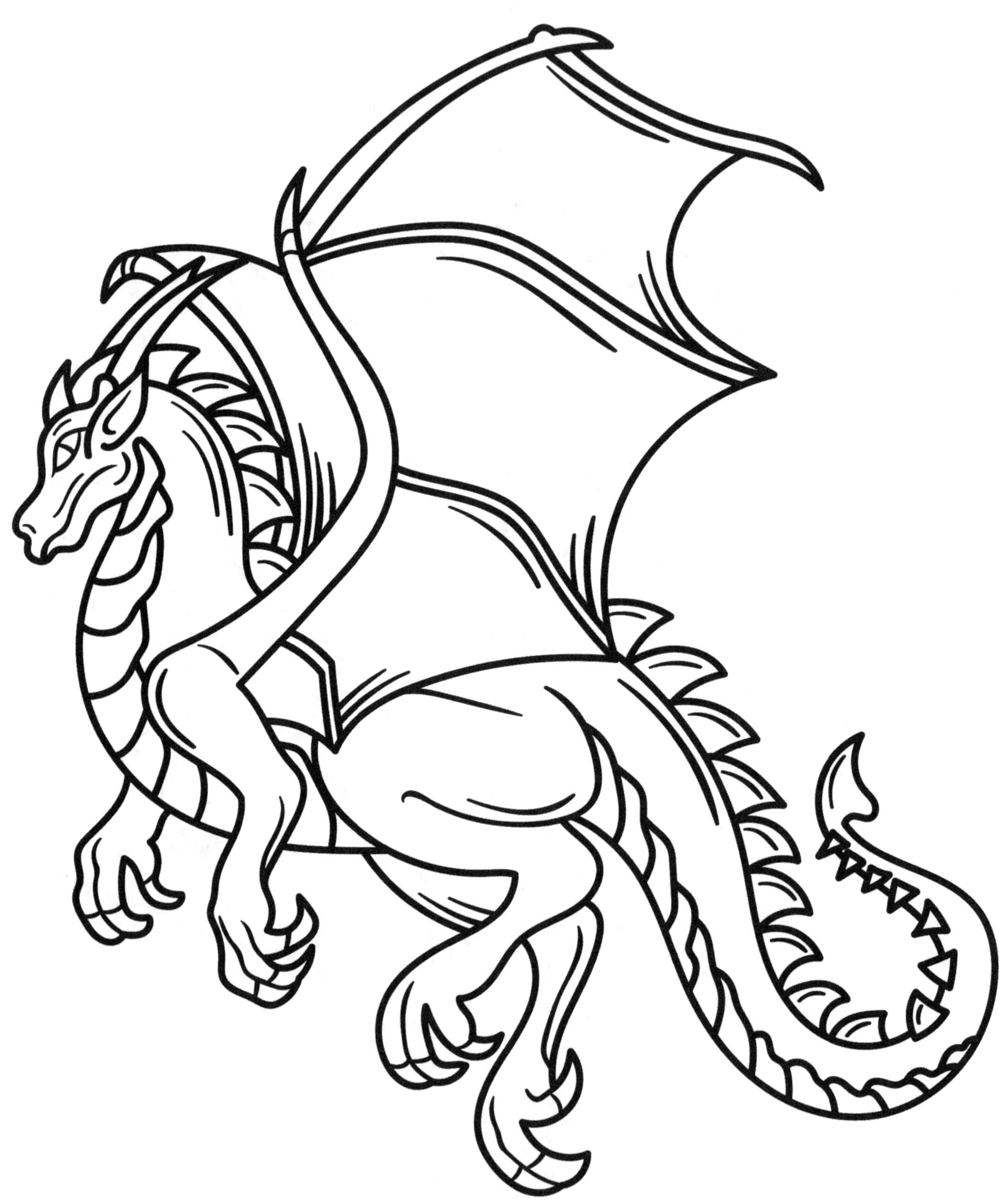

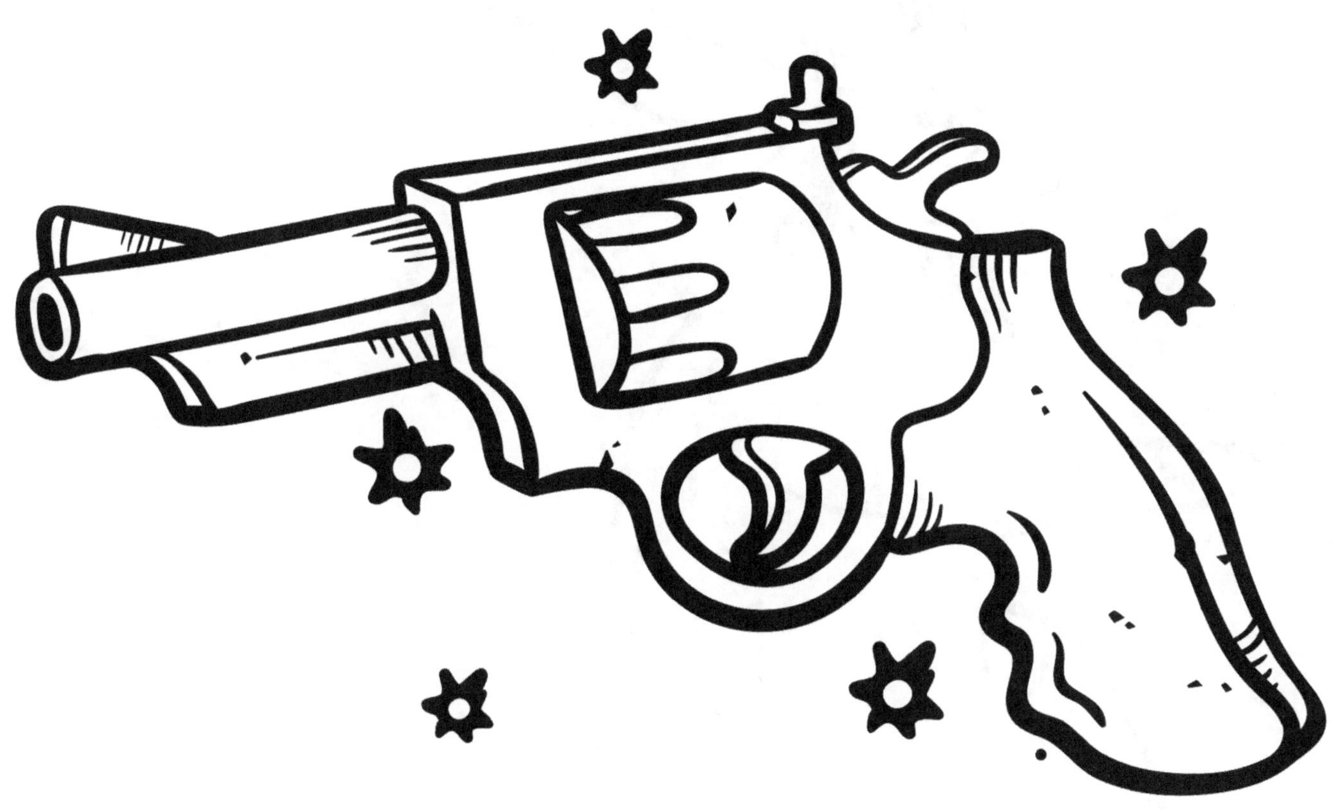

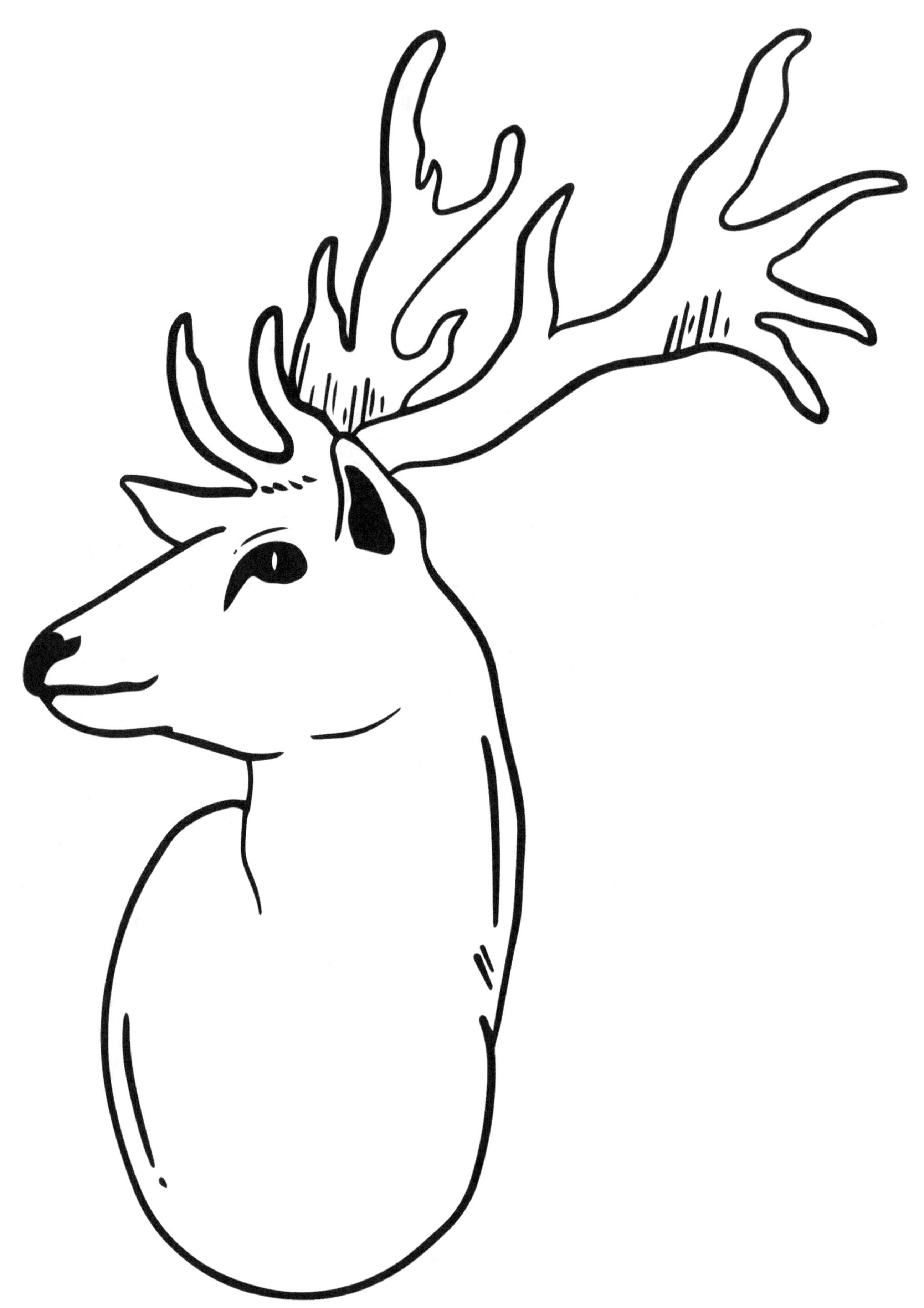

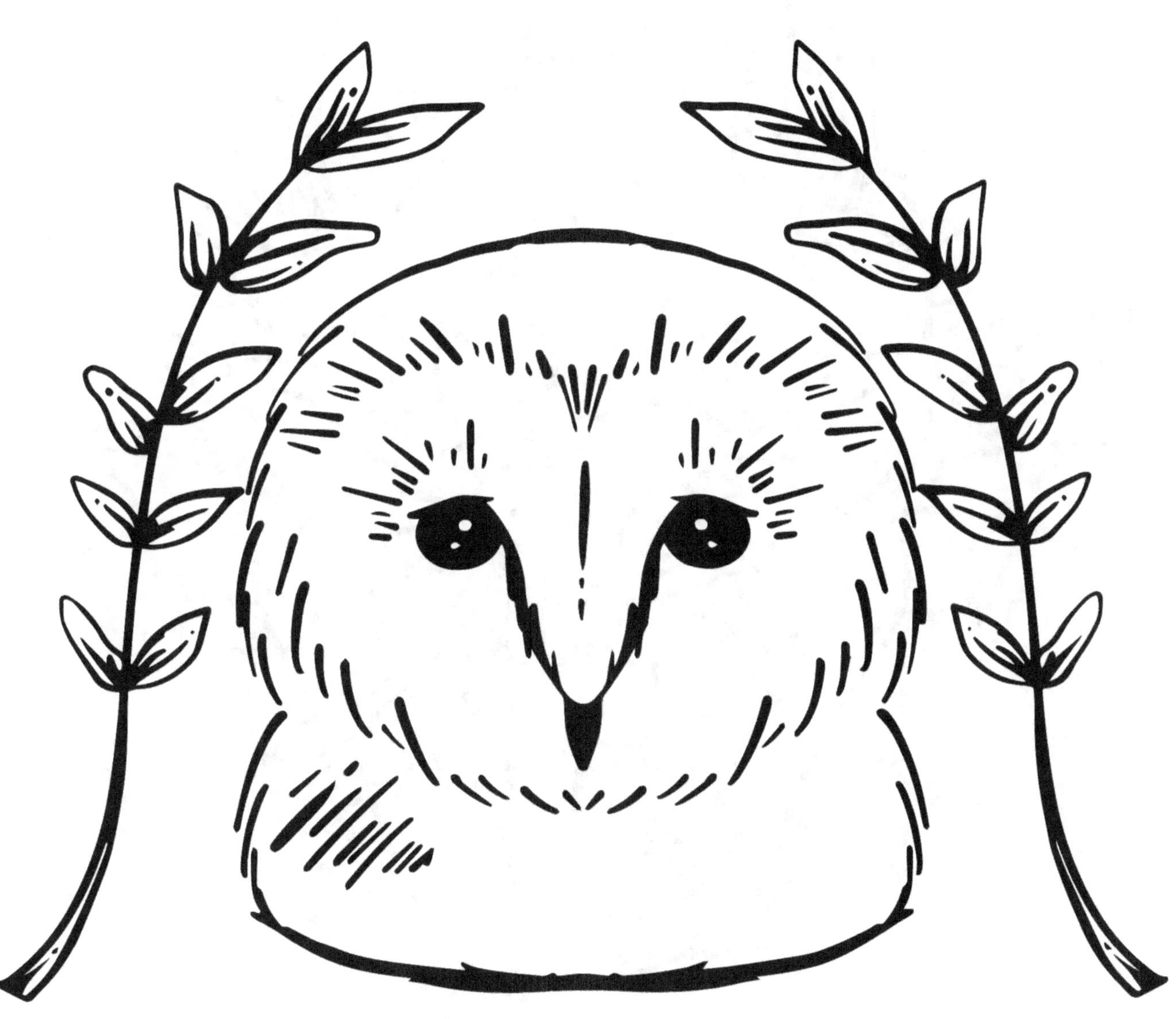

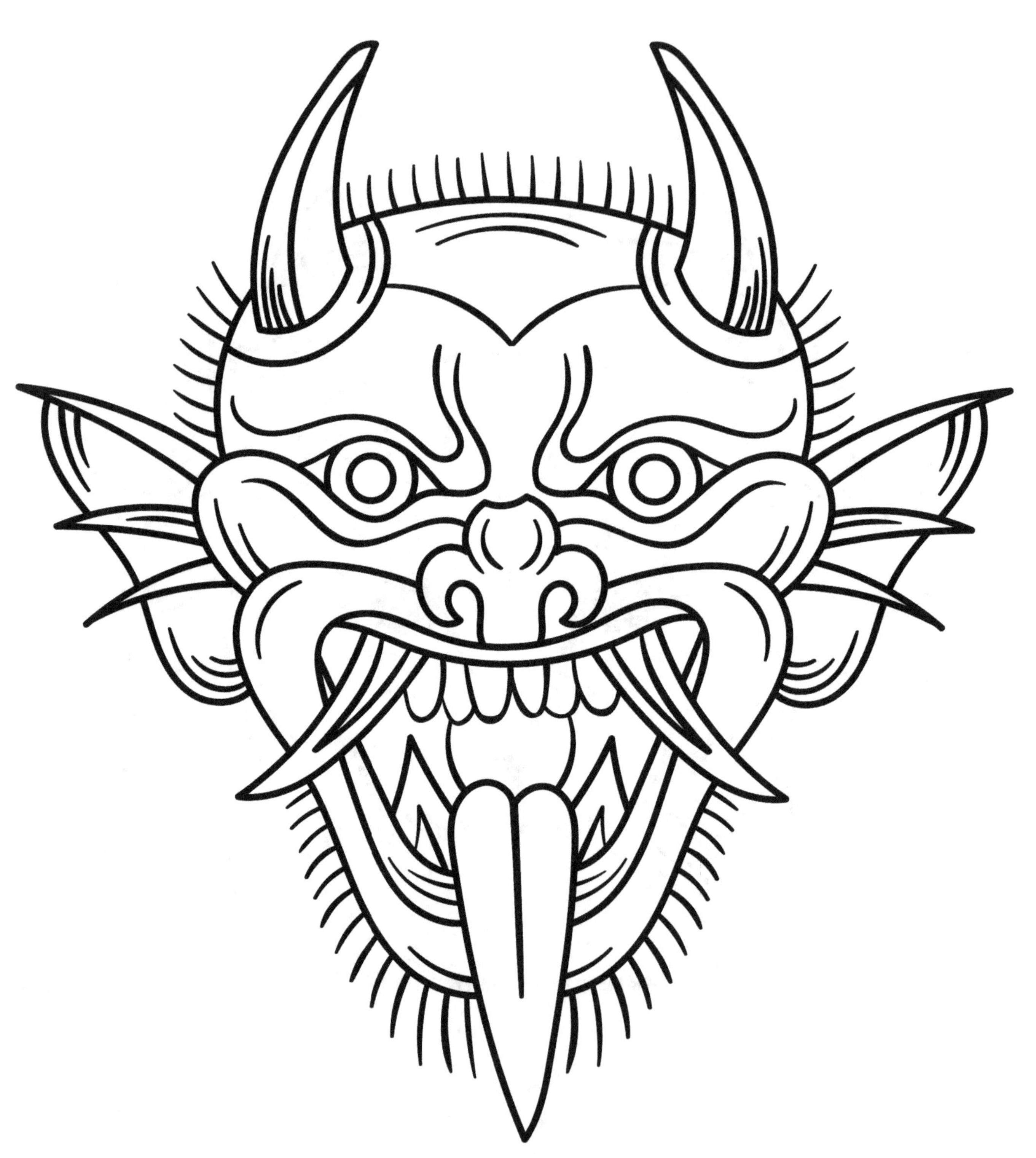

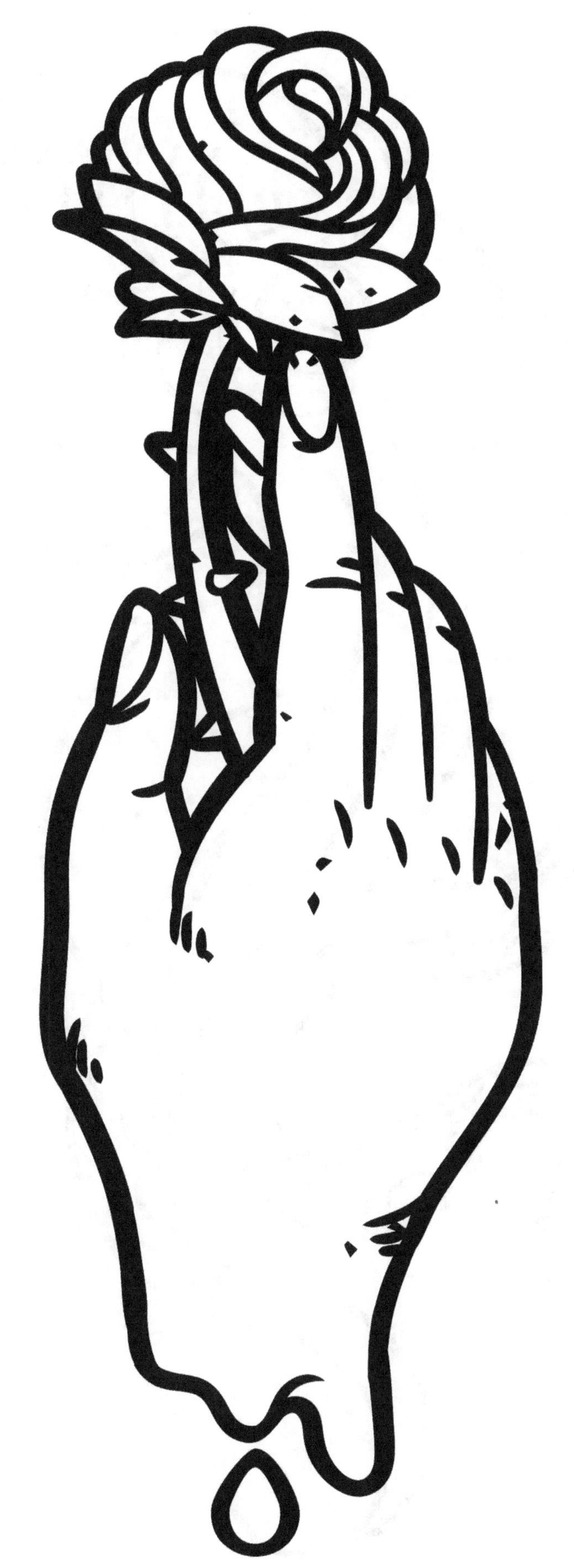

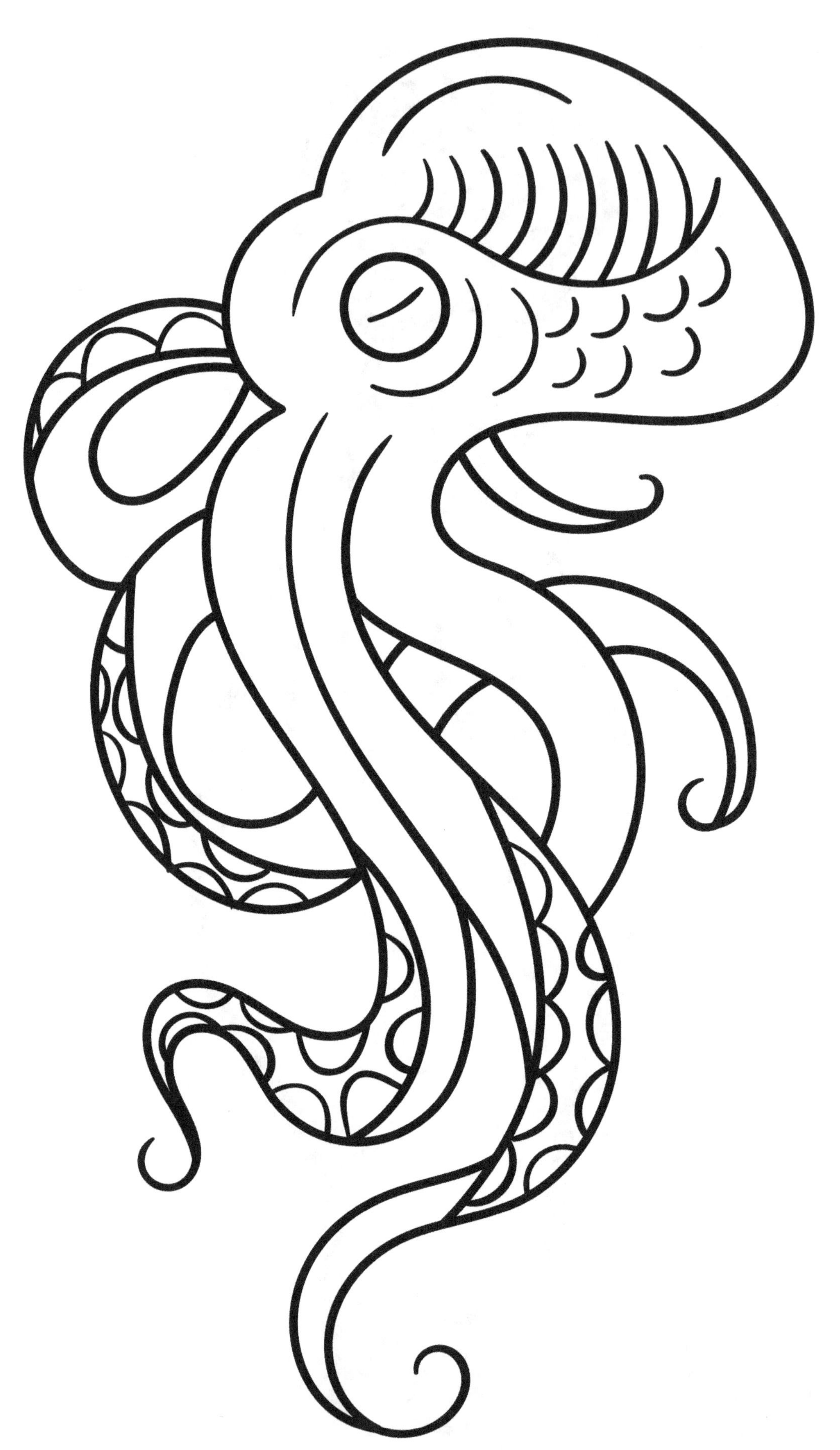

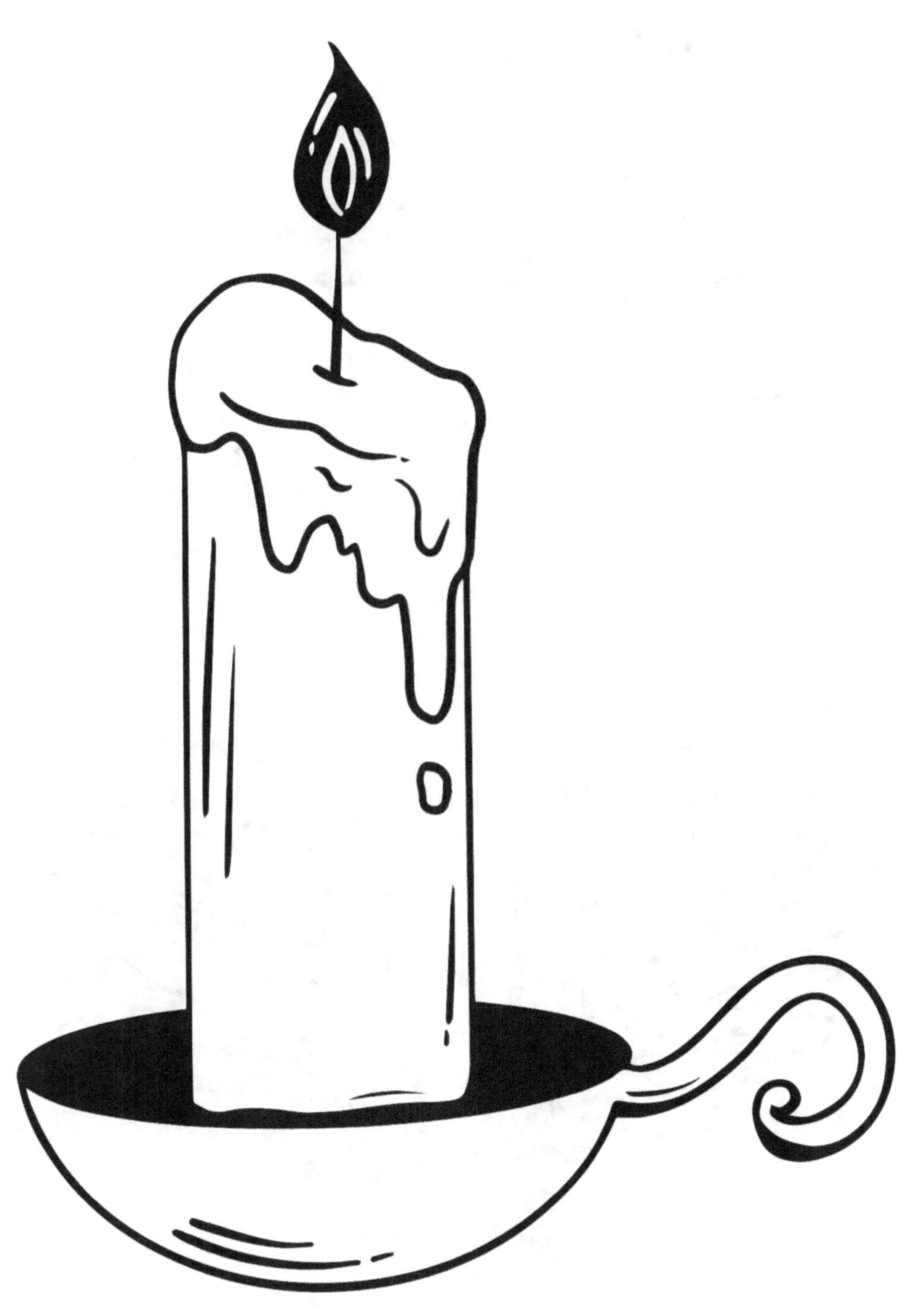

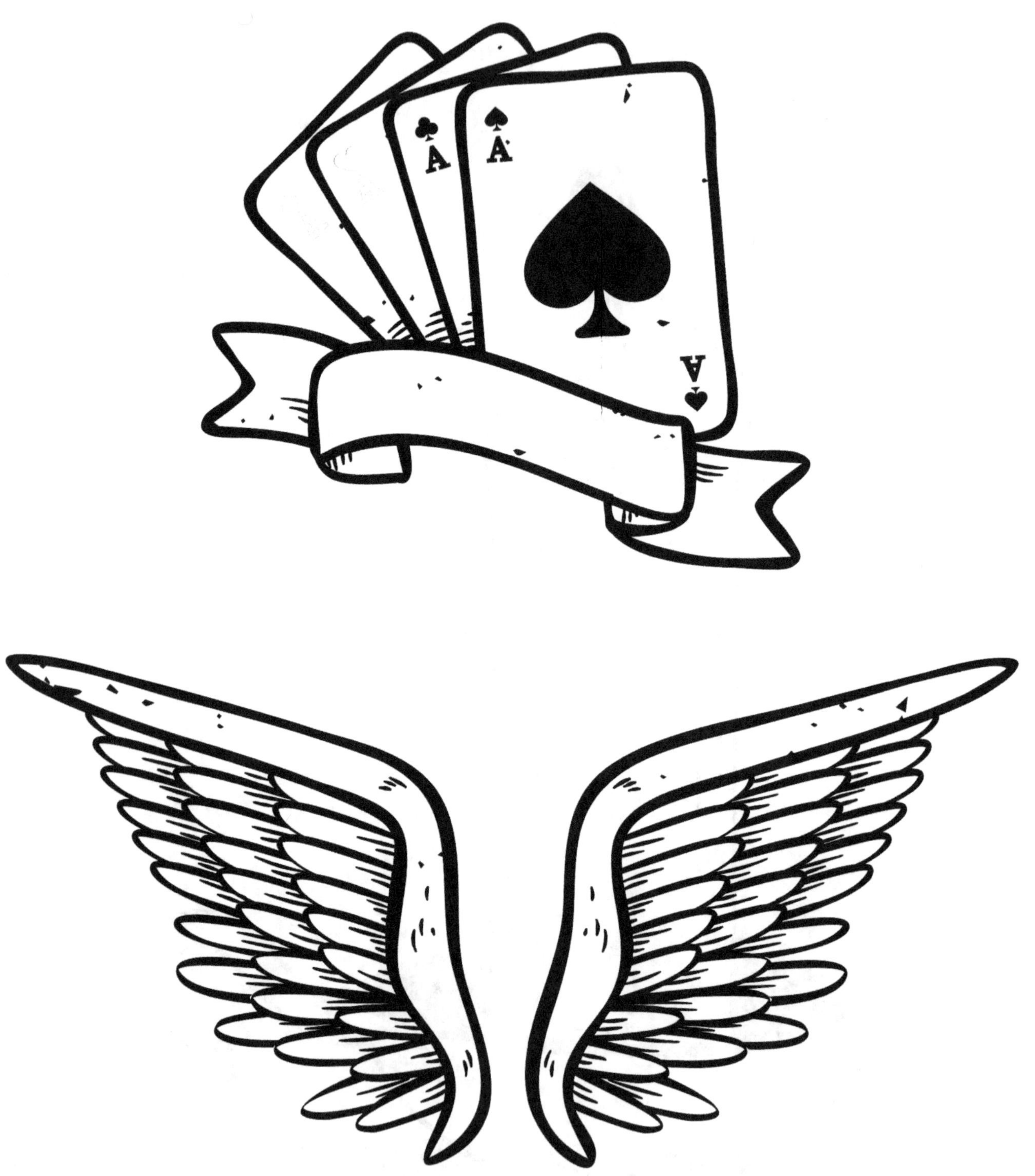

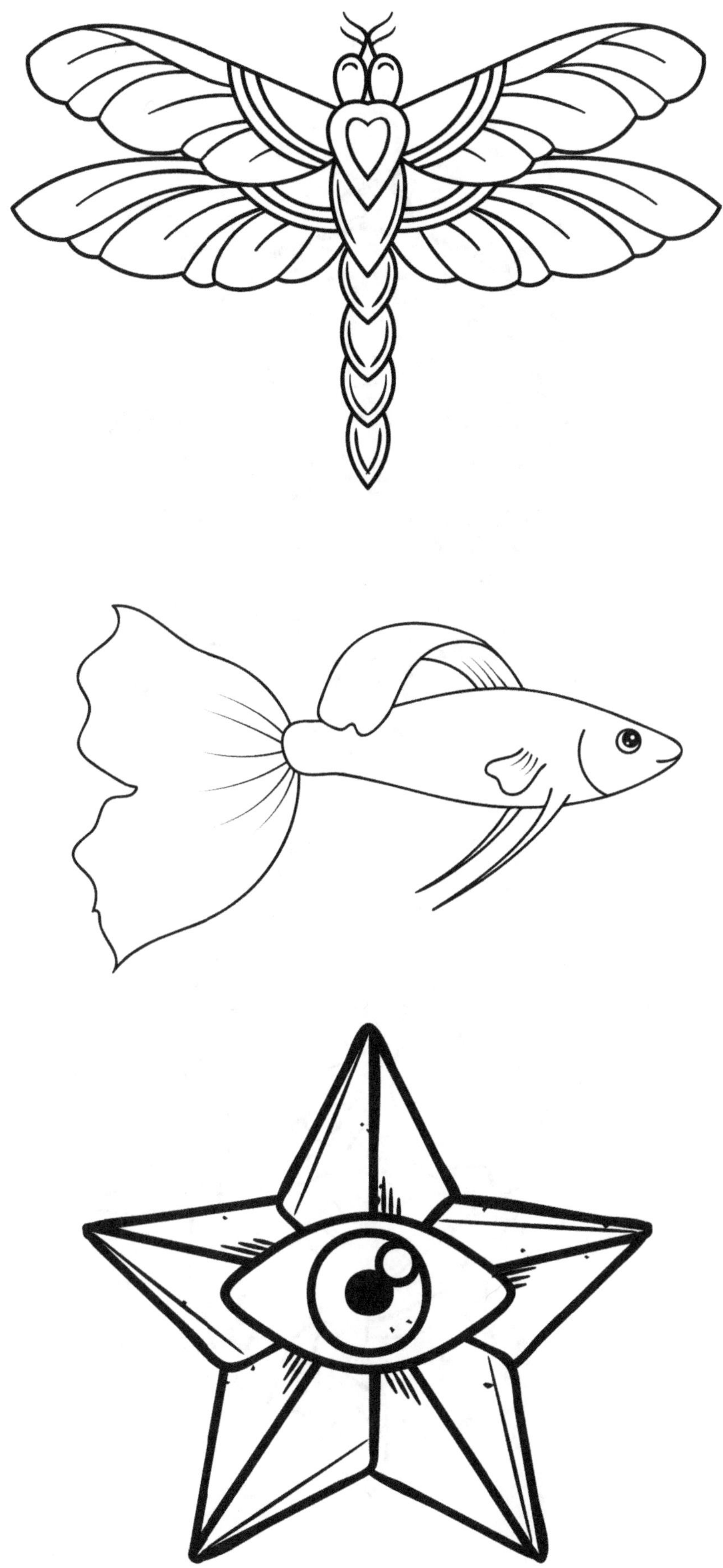

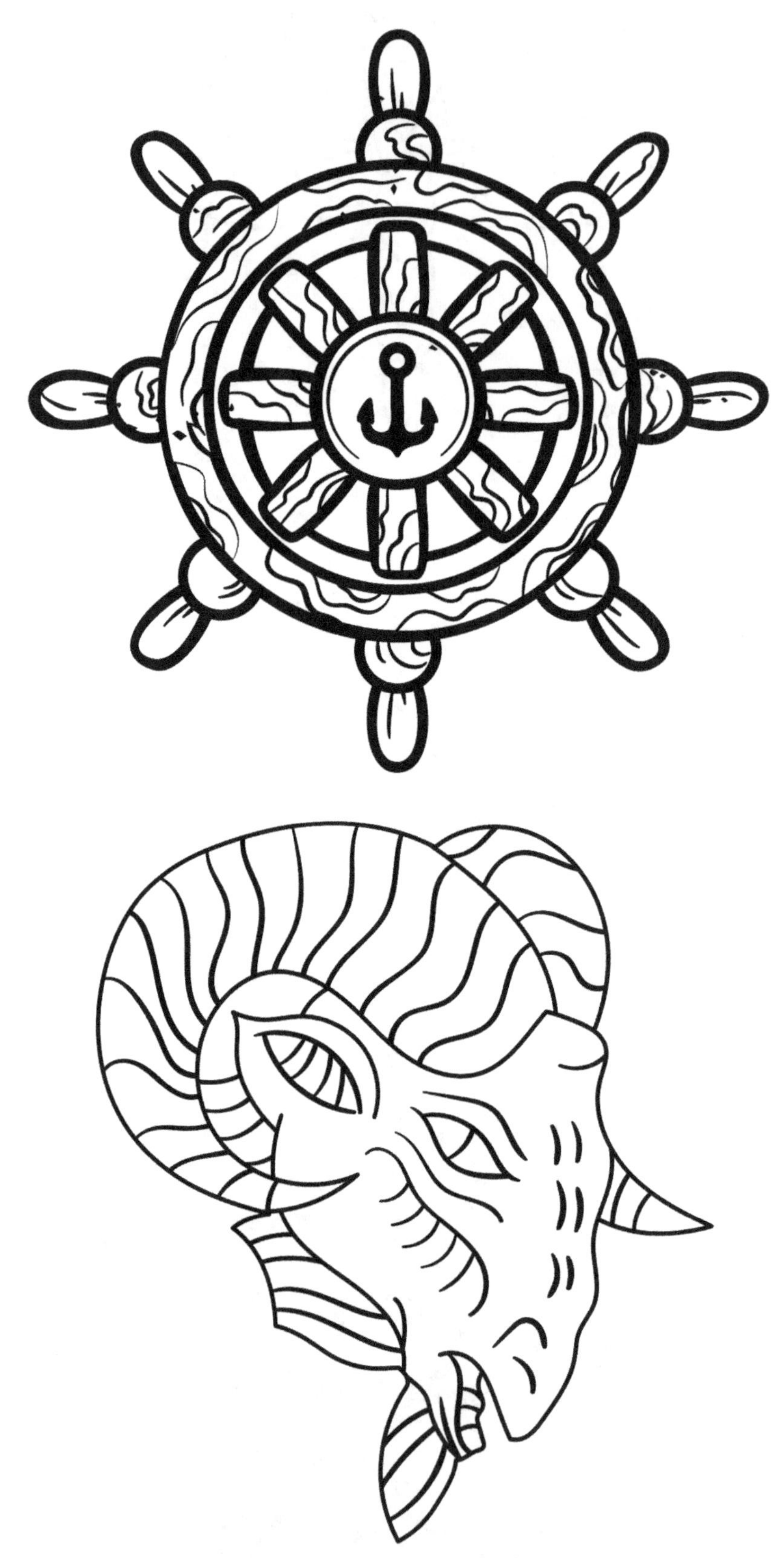

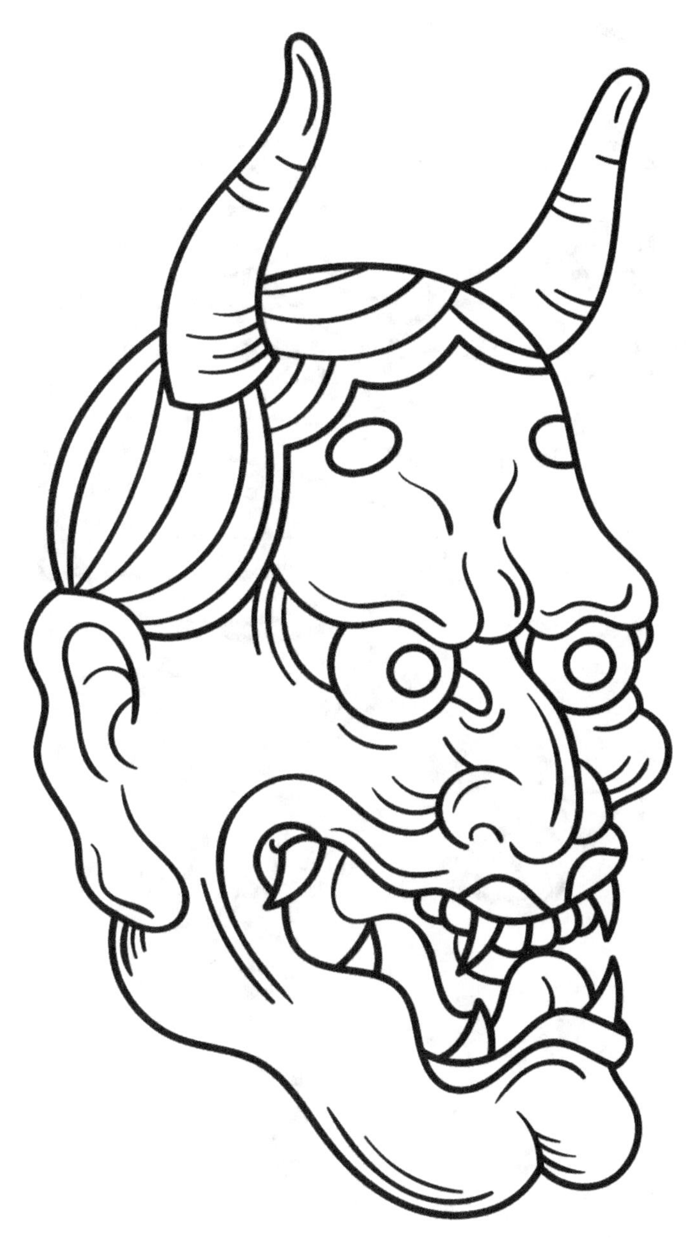

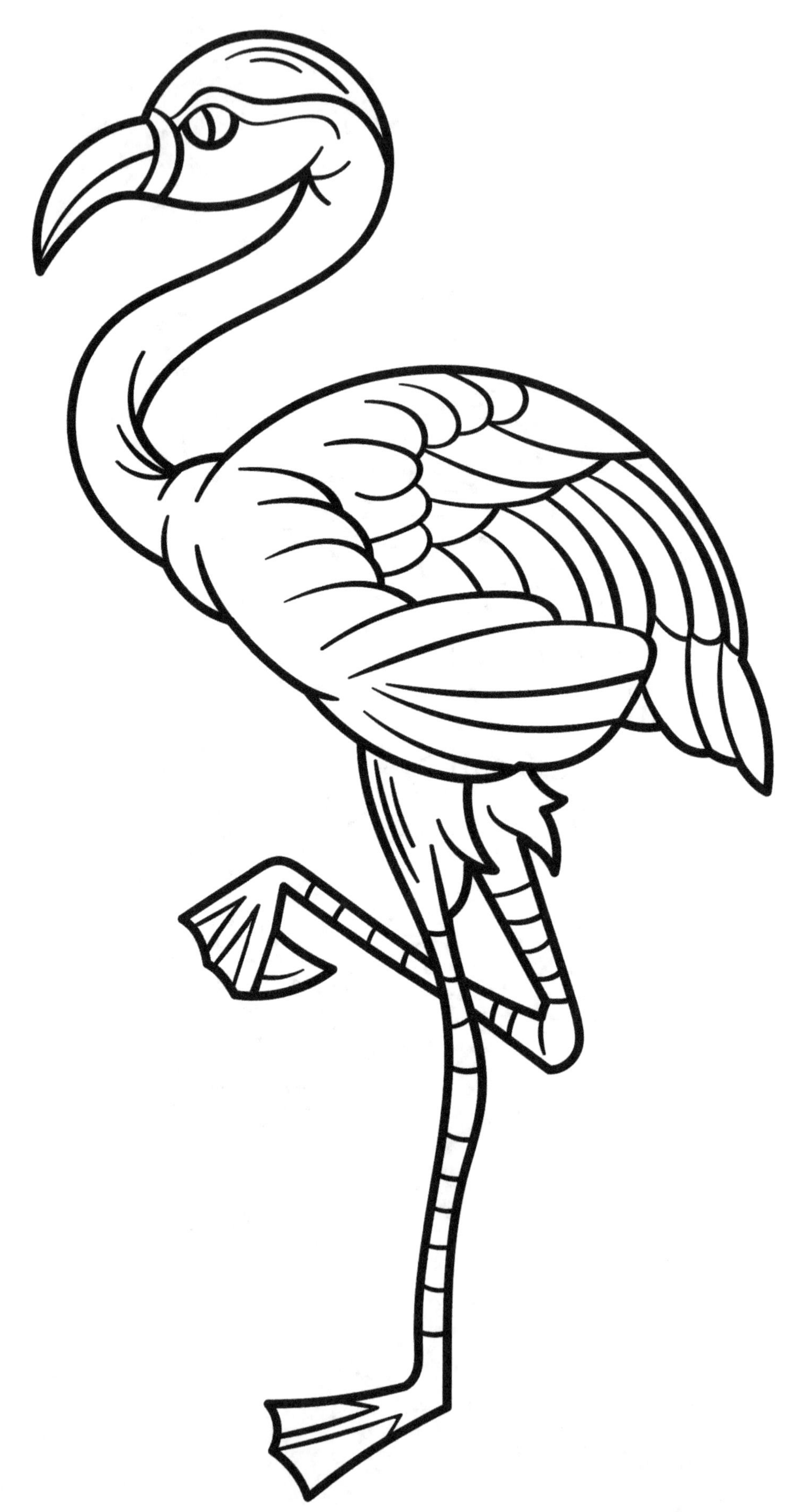

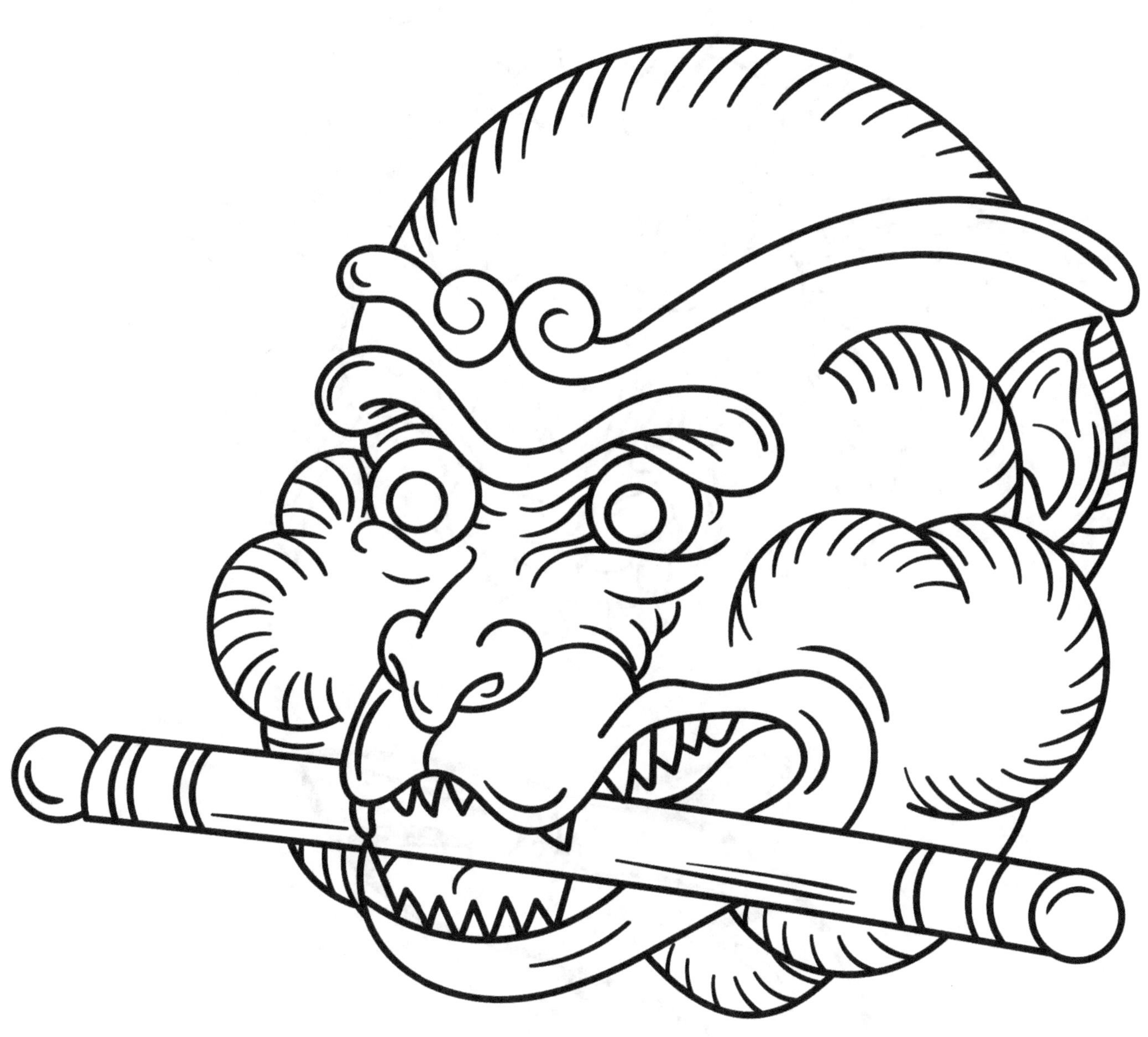

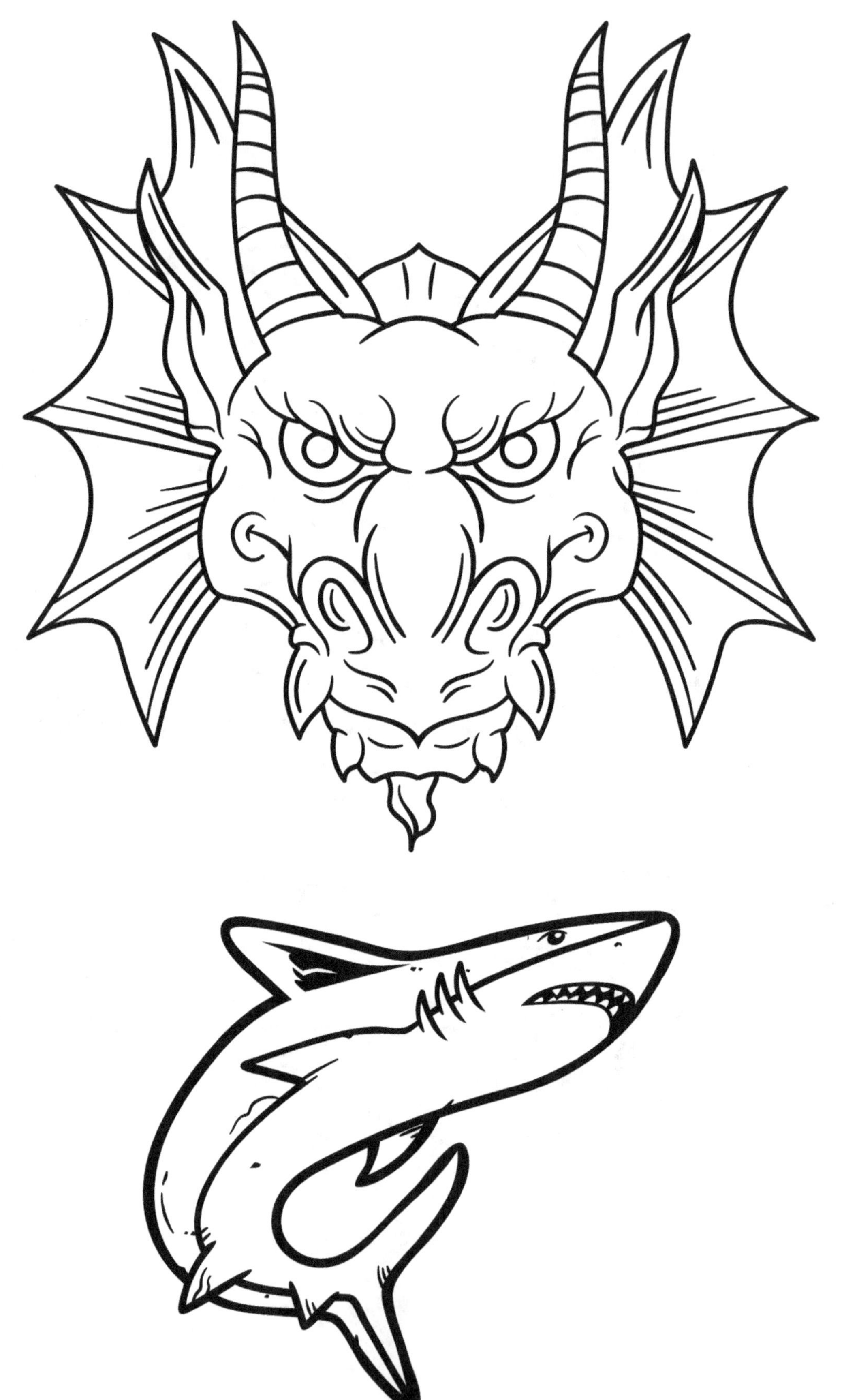

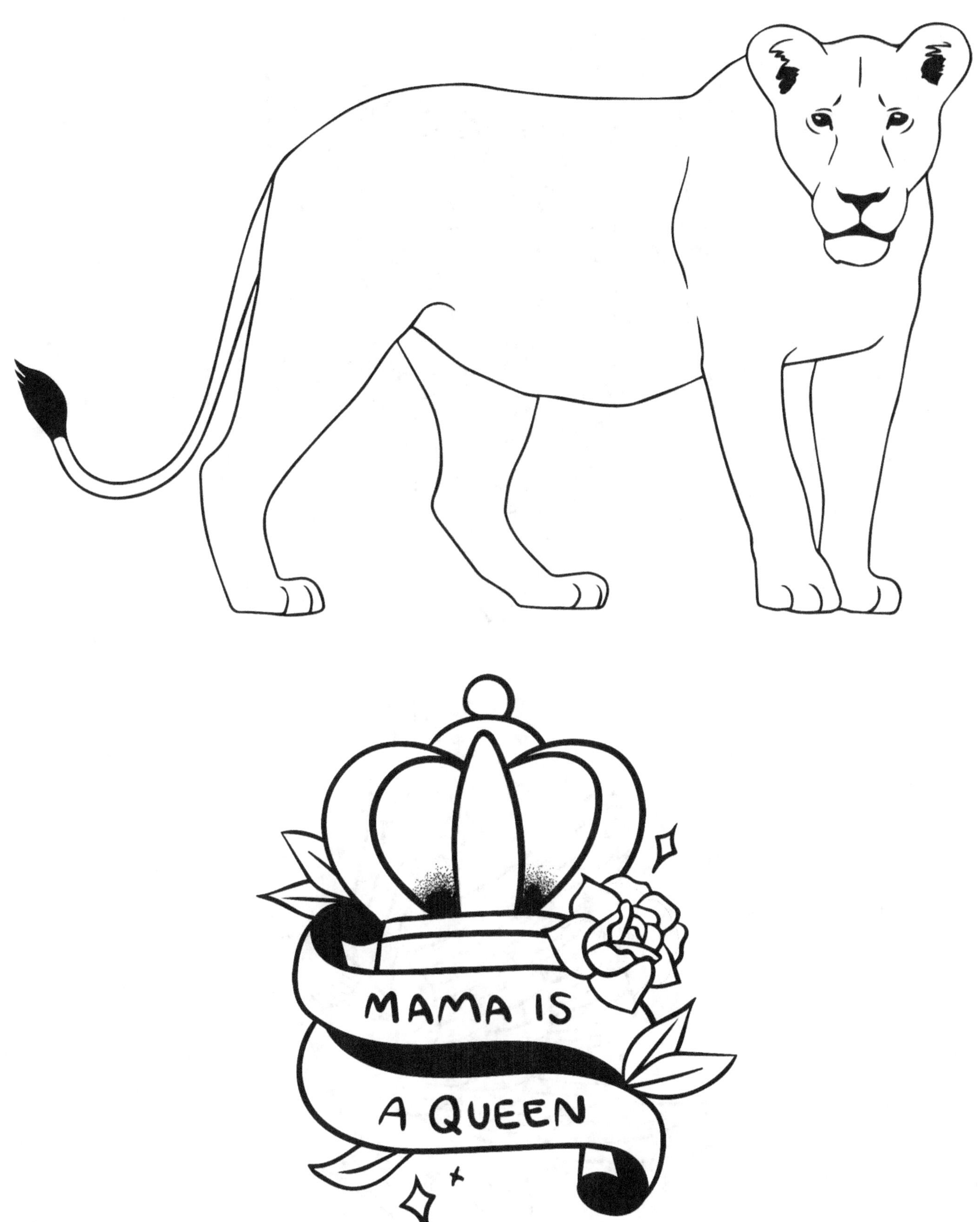
MAMA IS
A QUEEN

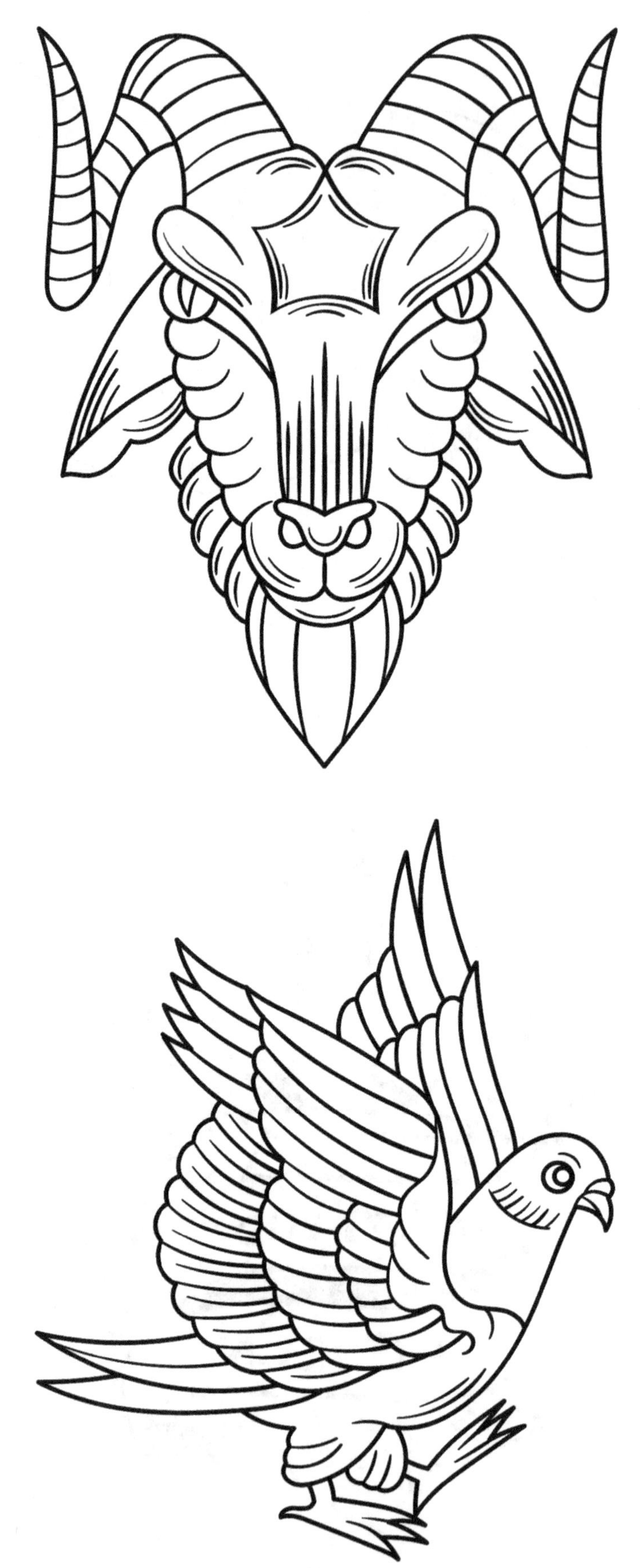

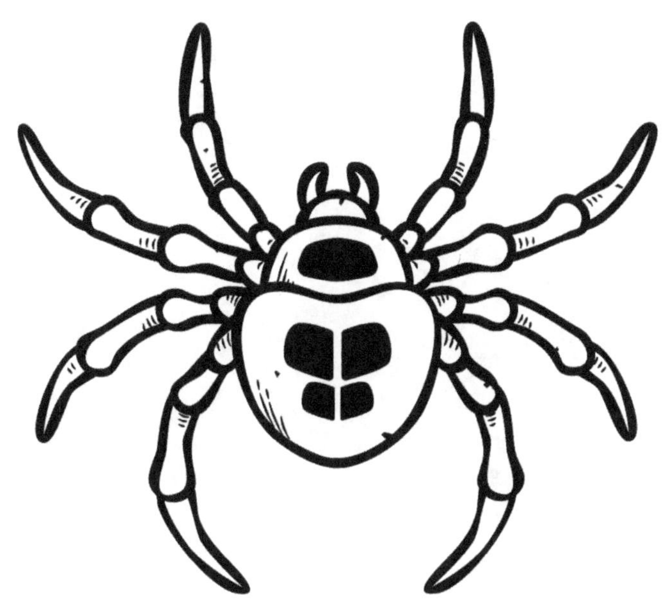

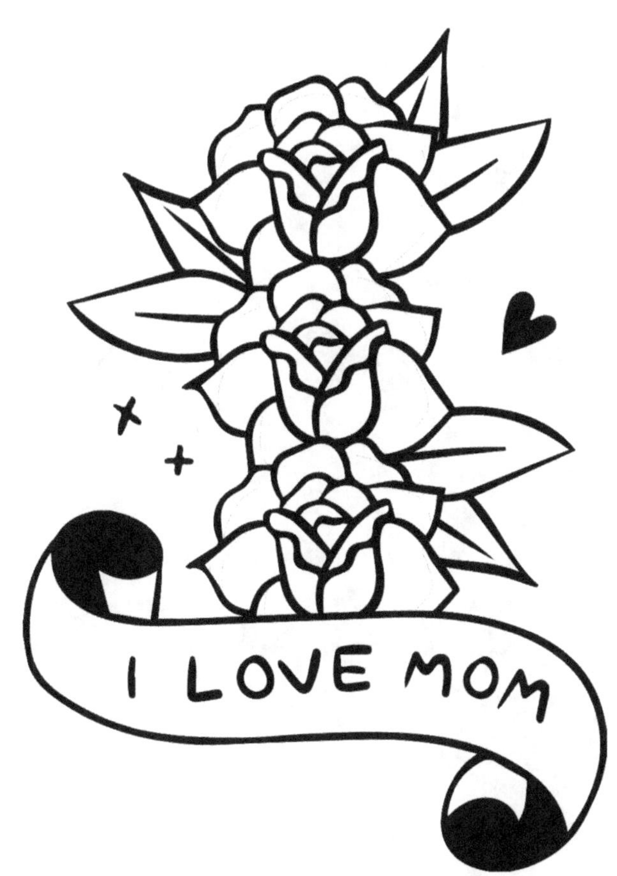
I LOVE MOM

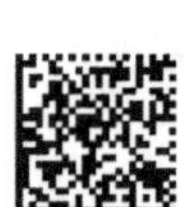
www.ingramcontent.com/pod-product-compliance
Lightning Source LLC
Chambersburg PA
CBHW080234260726
48658CB00008B/3098
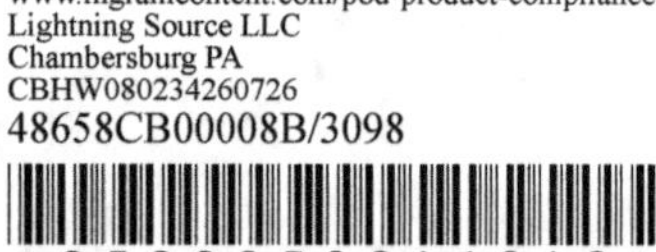